A GUIDE TO SANDWICH GLASS
WITCH BALLS, CONTAINERS AND TOYS

RAYMOND E. BARLOW
JOAN E. KAISER

PHOTOGRAPHS BY
  FORWARD'S COLOR PRODUCTIONS, INC.
  LEN LORETTE
  HUGO G. POISSON

EDITED BY LLOYD C. NICKERSON

BARLOW–KAISER PUBLISHING COMPANY, INC.

OTHER BOOKS BY RAYMOND E. BARLOW AND JOAN E. KAISER

The Glass Industry in Sandwich Volume 3
The Glass Industry in Sandwich Volume 4
A Guide to Sandwich Glass Vases, Colognes and Stoppers
A Guide to Sandwich Glass Candlesticks, Late Blown and Threaded
Barlow-Kaiser Sandwich Glass Price Guide

FORTHCOMING BOOKS BY RAYMOND E. BARLOW AND JOAN E. KAISER

The Glass Industry in Sandwich Volume 1
The Glass Industry in Sandwich Volume 2
The guides to Volumes 1 and 2 will contain:
  Whale oil and burning fluid lamps, with accessories
  Kerosene lamps and accessories
  Cup plates
  Lacy glass
  Blown molded glass
  Free-blown glass
  Pressed pattern tableware
  Salts
  Household items
  Cut, etched and engraved glass

A GUIDE TO SANDWICH GLASS
WITCH BALLS, CONTAINERS AND TOYS
First Edition

Copyright © 1987 by Raymond E. Barlow and Joan E. Kaiser

All correspondence and inquiries should be directed to

Barlow-Kaiser Publishing Co., Inc.
P.O. Box 265
Windham, NH 03087

in conjunction with

Schiffer Publishing Ltd.
1469 Morstein Road
West Chester, PA 19380

This book may be purchased from the publisher.

Try your bookstore first.

First Printing

Library of Congress Catalog Number
International Standard Book Number

Front cover: Photo 3260 Cavalier pomade jar, c. 1860.
Back cover: Photo 3261 Bear pomade jars, c. 1865. Photo 3361 Toy flat irons, c. 1860. Photo 3399 Epergne made by Nicholas J. Lutz, 1876. *Courtesy of The Bennington Museum, Bennington, Vermont.*
Spine: Photo 3411 Writing pen made by Nicholas J. Lutz, c. 1880.

INTRODUCTION

A book that will guide you when you are in the process of buying or appraising Sandwich glass is the most important tool you can own. This book is one of a series of guide books that describes every type of glass that was produced in Sandwich, Massachusetts. It uses the original plates of glass photos and the identification numbers from Volume 3 of *The Glass Industry in Sandwich*, a larger book by the same authors. (Volumes 3 and 4 are available, and Volumes 1 and 2 are in preparation.) This makes cross reference much easier.

In order to make this series of guides compact and light in weight, the photos from Volume 3 have been divided into two smaller guides. This one contains the complete chapters on witch balls, covered containers, toys (miniatures) and the creations of Nicholas Lutz. Another guide, available now, contains vases, colognes and stoppers.

The extensive categorization and illustration of Sandwich glass should make this guide valuable for field use. The prices in this guide reflect the market at the time of publication. They will be periodically updated in a separate price guide available from the publishers.

WHAT IS SANDWICH GLASS?

It is simple to define Sandwich glass. It was all glass that was produced within Sandwich, Massachusetts, a town on Cape Cod that was founded in 1637.

Glass production came to Sandwich in 1825, when Deming Jarves built and operated an enterprise that became world famous. He called it the Sandwich Glass Manufactory. It was incorporated as the Boston and Sandwich Glass Company in 1826. During the sixty-three years it was active, the factory produced an average of 100,000 pounds of glass per week. Yet this production was only *part* of the glass that should be attributed to Sandwich factories.

In 1859, the Cape Cod Glass Works began to manufacture glass. For ten years, this second factory produced 75,000 pounds of finished glassware each week in competition with the Boston and Sandwich Glass Company. When the works closed, production once again started up in 1883 in the buildings that had housed the Cape Cod Glass Works, under the name of the Vasa Murrhina Art Glass Company. Because of manufacturing difficulties, very little of their spangle and spatter glass reached the market. However, the pieces that can be documented should be given Sandwich attribution.

There were several later attempts to manufacture glass in Sandwich after the closing of the Boston and Sandwich Glass Company factory in 1888. In that year, a group of glassworkers built a small glass works and called themselves the Sandwich Co-operative Glass Company. This venture lasted only three years, but its existence cannot be ignored.

The Electrical Glass Corporation started production in 1890, followed by the Boston and Sandwich Glass Company II, the Boston and Sandwich Glass Company III, and the Sandwich Glass Company. The Alton Manufacturing Company was the last to produce glass on this site. Its most notable product resembled Tiffany glass and was called Trevaise. Like its predecessors, the Alton Manufacturing Company was short-lived, and in 1908, glass was no longer manufactured in Sandwich. *But the glass made by these small companies deserves to be called Sandwich glass because it was made in Sandwich, Massachusetts.*

There were several other companies in Sandwich that worked on glass but did not make it. They cut it, etched it, engraved it, decorated it, and assembled it. The glass that they worked on, called *blanks*, was brought to Sandwich from factories in Pennsylvania. Regardless of what was done to the surface of this Pennsylvania product, *it cannot be called Sandwich glass.* Only glass that is shaped while hot can be attributed to a particular factory.

This book deals only with the glass that was manufactured in Sandwich and is therefore entitled to be called Sandwich glass.

WHICH BALLS ARE WITCH BALLS?

1825–1887

One of the simplest forms to make out of glass is a ball. A glob of hot glass is gathered on the end of a blowpipe and the blowpipe is rotated slowly as the ball is inflated. Depending on its use, it may be allowed to cool naturally or may be sent to the leer and cooled slowly to eliminate stress in the glass.

Some of the earliest of these round pieces also had necks and were used to hold holy water. A knob on the end of the neck allowed the primitive bottle to be hung. It was common belief that such bottles with their contents provided protection against evil spirits. Such spirits, from mischievous fairies to evil witches, were feared for their ability to cause sickness, deformities, and even death to both man and beast. In America, this fear culminated in the nightmare of witch-hangings in Salem, Massachusetts—a black chapter during the early years of the colonies.

Witches were thought to fear certain herbs and, strangely, "roundness". Logically, herbs placed in a sphere would provide a double whammy. One theory had it that evil beings were attracted to herbs. By placing herbs in a ball, witches might be dissuaded from bothering the occupants of a house or barn, or perhaps the witch would enter the ball instead and become trapped in a tangle of leaves and twigs, rendering it harmless. Either way, whether the balls were needed to trap the witch or ward it off, early glass companies had a ready market for such mystical devices.

By the early 1800's, a glass works at Nailsea in the Bristol area of England, was producing balls that could be filled with herbs to counteract the havoc of the unknown. The first of these were made of clear glass, crudely splashed with specks of blue and white. Soon after, designs of crude loopings and swirls were developed. The practice of making witch balls spread to other glass houses throughout England and across the sea to the New World. Within sixty days of the incorporation of the Boston and Sandwich Glass Company, witch balls were being produced. The document known as the *sloar book* (called a *turn book* by some students) shows that on May 20, 1826, 170 witch balls were made. They were 2½" in diameter, and in sub-

sequent entries would be described as "small". On May 27, 1826, fifty-six 3½" witch balls were made, later to be entered as "large" witch balls. Throughout 1827 and into 1828, witch balls made up a surprisingly large part of production. Most were made in the shop headed by Michael Doyle.

So far as is known, all Sandwich witch balls were made to be hung. There is no indication in the sloar book that matching witch ball stands were manufactured, or are there fragments dug at the site that could be identified as such. The balls were hung by inserting a small piece of wood into the same hole used to fill the ball with herbs. The piece of wood was carved into a peg with a notch around the center. One end of a ribbon, string or wire was tied around the notch, and the peg was inserted into the ball and placed horizontally across the hole. The ball could then be hung in any location.

Local tradition may have determined the purpose of the various types of witch balls. In the Cape Cod area, decorative witch balls made by the Boston and Sandwich Glass Company were meant to be hung in houses—on porches, in windows, and even in bedrooms to protect children. Some were made of spatter glass, but most were a marbrie design of four loopings. Four types of marbrie fragments known to be from witch balls were dug at the factory site—clear with white loopings, clear with pink loopings, white with pink loopings, and clear with alternating pink and white loopings. The loopings divide the ball into four parts. Witch balls blown in a single color were meant to be hung in barns to protect livestock. They can be found in amber, amethyst, blue, green, even white, and are quite heavy.

Single color witch balls blown in South Jersey that had matching stands were obviously made to be used in houses. It certainly would not have been practical to use a ball on a stand in an outbuilding. But these were made in areas with different traditions from Sandwich.

A fifth type of marbrie design fragment dug at the site was made from a gather of opaque white glass with red and blue loopings. Many of the red, white and blue balls were *militia balls*. They were an outgrowth of the tampion, a wood plug or stopper put in the muzzle of a gun not in use. After the Civil War, it was the custom for men who were in the militia to march in holiday parades. They were in uniform and carried muskets in an upright position alongside their leg. The bayonet was reversed on the musket. If the men were glassworkers or were escorting glassworkers, they placed a red, white and blue glass ball on the muzzle end of the musket. The balls were up to five inches in diameter and had a long glass rod-like extension that was inserted into the barrel. This was done at Sandwich for several years on the Fourth of July, and the *Crockery Journal* dated June 24, 1875, provides us with a colorful description of New England Glass Company workers marching in the Bunker Hill celebration parade on June 17.

> In the procession there appeared a creditable display of glass companies and kindred establishments, foremost among which was the New England Glass Company. First came as escort the "Coventry Cadets" of Cambridge — 45 men headed by a drum corps, each soldier carrying in the muzzle of his musket a glass globe, the three colors, red, white and blue, being so distributed as to produce a pleasing effect.

If you find what you believe to be a red, white and blue witch ball with the remains of a glass plug extension, you very likely have found a militia ball. The workmanship is not good. No time was taken to make even loopings.

Similar balls, made with a tapered extension and in a single color, were made by the Boston and Sandwich Glass Company and the New England Glass Company. The January 20, 1855, issue of *Ballou's Pictorial* illustrates several of them in the New England Glass Company showroom. Mounted on tall standards, they could be used as single-unit apothecary show globes. The Boston and Sandwich Glass Company made them to use at trade exhibitions. To delineate the perimeter of the space allotted the glass company, and to keep the public a safe distance from the glass-laden tables, a curb was nailed together out of wood. The top boards had evenly spaced large holes to accept the extensions of the balls. The side boards were high enough to cover the lower half of each ball. After the balls were inserted, the space between each ball and the side boards was filled with confetti. At one particular exhibition, green balls alternated with white ones, and green and white confetti filled the spaces. The judges were impressed by how much the colorful curb added to the decor of the booth.

After the trade show was over, the decoration balls were piled in the Boston showroom and soon were being used as handled cover balls for wide-mouthed store jars. Today, all of our candy and over-the-counter medicine is sealed against contamination. In the Nineteenth Century, bacteria and viruses were not understood, and a storekeeper handled everything with his bare hands. Extremely large jars that could hold two or three gallons were used for dispensing pills, liquid medicines and candy. The mouth of the jars was wide enough for a man's arm, so that he could twist his elbow inside the jar to scoop or ladle from the very bottom.

When the jars were originally purchased from the glass companies, they had a glass cover with a knob-like finial. The cover had an inside flange that was machined to fit tightly against the inside of the neck of the jar, like the plug of a stopper. This original cover did not lend itself to rapid, constant use. The tight fit prevented evaporation, but the cover chipped when it was hurriedly replaced, causing slivers of glass to fall into the jar. The leftover

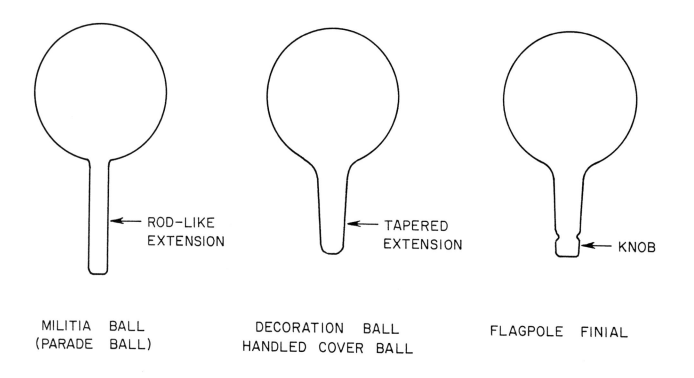

MILITIA BALL
(PARADE BALL)

DECORATION BALL
HANDLED COVER BALL

FLAGPOLE FINIAL

trade show decoration balls with their easy-to-grasp tapered extensions made perfect handled cover balls. A busy merchant could remove and replace them rapidly, and the round balls did not chip.

It was a custom in Sandwich to mount ruby glass balls on the tops of flagpoles, where their reflection on a sunny day could be seen some distance away. Balls that were intended for flagpole finials had a knob on the end of the extension so that they could be set in plaster without pulling out, either directly into a hole drilled into the end of the pole or into a metal fitting that was mounted on the pole. We do not know whether this custom was only a local one or if it extended to other glass factory villages.

Lastly, our discussion of balls with extensions should include the ball that was the uppermost unit of a Sandwich apothecary show globe. Show globes are large jars that were placed in store windows to indicate the presence of a druggist. Many people could not read. They depended on figural symbols, such as the spiral striped pole of a barber. Show globes were made up of several jar units, one above the other, each with a plug extension that was inserted into the neck of the unit directly below it. Part of the extension rested flatly on the lip of the lower unit, as seen in the illustration. This provided stability for each unit, necessary because most show globes were made from clear glass and were filled with colored water.

Any of these balls could be mistaken for a witch ball if the extension was broken off, and several of these forms—especially in smaller sizes—could be mistaken for a darning ball.

Balls with an opening were also used for target shooting, much as the clay pigeon is used today. The balls were filled with anything that would be visible when they were shattered by a bullet, such as feathers, confetti, or cotton.

No time was spent in their manufacture because they were for one-time use only. The opening is generally jagged, and the glass from which they were produced was made primarily from cullet. This accounts for their great variety of colors—apple green, light blue, and several shades of amber. Fragments that we have been able to identify as target balls were blown into a mold that is dated October 23, 1877, and carries the name of its patentee, Ira Paine, in a band circling the center. Paine's target ball was also found in excavations at a New York glass house, indicating that the mold was a private one sent to any house that gave a low bid. Fragments dug at Sandwich indicate that the Boston and Sandwich Glass Company must have been low bidder at least once.

Two types of *closed* balls without extensions were made at the Boston and Sandwich Glass Company. First, thick-walled blown balls were used as covers on pitchers, bowls and store jars. They were weighted at the pontil end to keep them from rolling and were annealed for strength. Second, free-blown balls with thin walls were produced not as a saleable item but for packing. They were placed upon vases as a support for the rims during shipment. This important factory practice was discovered at the dig site. The remains of a wooden case were uncovered with twelve blown trumpet vases inside, all damaged. Six vases were canary in color, six were amethyst. Two of the canary vases had canary balls still in perfect condition placed on the vase openings, showing how the vases had been packed in the case.

Author Ray Barlow and fellow Sandwich historian Francis (Bill) Wynn experimented with this technique in 1968, using Tappan vases from the Late Blown Period. They placed twelve vases in a wooden box and packed salt marsh hay around them just as the factory did. Packing

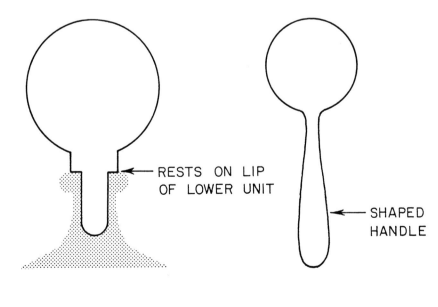

TOP UNIT OF
SHOW GLOBE

DARNING BALL

RESTS ON LIP OF LOWER UNIT

SHAPED HANDLE

Fig. 12 Identifying features of blown balls with extensions. Militia balls are multi-colored, with a rod-like extension that fits into the muzzle of a musket. Decoration balls left over from trade exhibitions were used as jar covers. The tapered extension made a comfortable handle. Balls used on the tops of flagpoles were blown with a knob on the end, not unlike early holy water bottles. Apothecary globe units have extensions that fit into the neck of a lower unit, but are shaped to rest flatly on top of the lower unit. Some of these forms resemble darning balls, but a darning ball has a shaped handle.

balls were placed on six of the vases, while six other vases were left with their rims uncovered. The packed case was placed in the back of a station wagon and left there for two weeks, assuming that two weeks of normal driving would equal one trip from Sandwich to Boston in an 1850 horse-drawn wagon. When the box was opened, the salt marsh hay had settled into and around the vases without the balls, exposing the rims. The hay had not moved around the vases with the balls. Any rough treatment to the box would have rendered the vases without packing balls vulnerable to damage. The vases with balls would have been able to sustain abusive treatment and still would have arrived at their destination intact.

When looking for such balls to add to your collection, understand that they were meant to last only until the vases were unpacked. They are paper-thin and were not annealed. As long as pressure was maintained evenly on all areas of their surface, they had strength. When separated from the vase they were blown to fit, their strength was lost and they shattered more easily than an eggshell, particularly if the air inside expanded from the heat of your hand. Because they were blown bubble-thin, their pigment is barely visible, even though the balls and the vases were made from the same color glass.

There are available on the antiques market large quantities of glass balls made in Japan. Some are used for decorative purposes, others were made to be used as floats for fishing nets. The openings of these balls are closed with a separate glob of glass that is forced into the opening while the ball is still hot. This permanently seals the opening, making the ball airtight. This method of closing the ball was not used at Sandwich. Sandwich glass balls used as covers and for packing were closed as they were broken from the blowpipe.

THESE SIMPLE HINTS WILL HELP YOU IDENTIFY SANDWICH GLASS BALLS.

Glass balls made in Sandwich do not have their openings plugged with a separate glob of glass.

Marbrie witch ball fragments dug at the factory site are clear with white loopings, clear with pink loopings, white with pink loopings, and clear with alternating white and pink loopings. The loopings divide the ball into quarters.

Witch balls used to protect animals in outbuildings are of one color and very heavy.

Militia balls are similar to marbrie witch balls, but have a long glass plug extension that is the same diameter its entire length. If you find a red, white and blue ball with an exceptionally rough opening, with the remains of a glass rod-like extension, you have a militia ball.

Balls used for decoration and as handled covers are a single color, are heavy and have a tapered extension.

Balls mounted on flagpoles are heavy and have a knob on the end of the extension.

Apothecary show globe units have an extension that partly rests on a lower unit. The remainder of the extension is a plug that fits into the neck of a lower unit.

Balls without extensions used as covers are heavy, are weighted on the pontil end to prevent rolling and have no opening.

Packing balls were blown very thin, are of one color, and were not annealed. They have no opening.

Target balls marked "IRA PAINE" and dated October 23, 1877, were made at Sandwich, and also at other factories. They are one color.

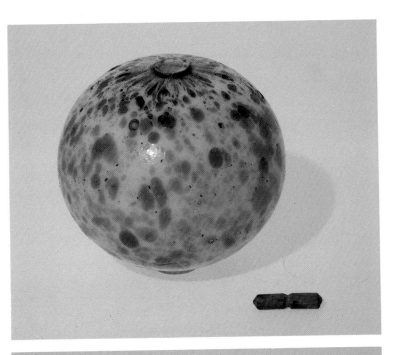

3225 WITCH BALL
3½" Dia. 1830–1840

This witch ball may be the earliest one shown in this chapter. It was blown using opaque white glass as the basic color, and, while molten, was rolled over fragments of red and blue glass. The ball cooled so rapidly that the colored pieces did not melt into the white. The surface, therefore, remained rough and jagged. This ball is one of four in the collection of a Cape Cod family descended from a Sandwich worker. The four original wood peg hangers accompanying the balls are ¾" to 1¼" long. Their diameter varies depending on the diameter of the hole into which they were inserted. "Art glass" type witch balls were meant for household use.

3226 WITCH BALL
3½" Dia. 1840–1850

This ball was found on Cape Cod with its original hanger. It has family ties to a Sandwich worker and was used in a house. There is no question about how this spatter glass piece was made. The clear glass ball was started on the end of a blowpipe. Pieces of broken red and white glass were spread on the marver. While the clear glass was still hot, it was rolled over the colored pieces. They melted into the clear glass and became a part of the ball. Some of the red pieces did not adhere properly, and can be picked out, leaving a clear indentation such as can be seen on the upper left edge.

3227 WITCH BALLS
4" Dia. 1850–1870

All of the marbrie witch ball fragments dug at the site of the Boston and Sandwich Glass Company have a four-loop configuration. The ends of all of the loops are at the opening of the ball. The loops are well defined, but vary in size. Multi-colored (called *parti-colored* in the 1800's) witch balls were used in dwellings. It was believed that hanging them over the entrance door stopped evil spirits at the threshold, and they would enter the ball instead of the house.

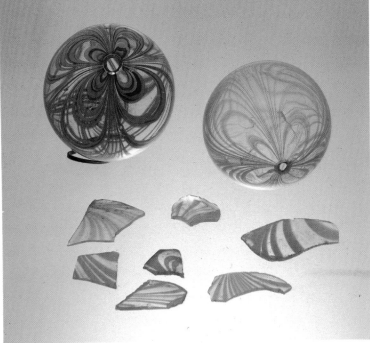

3228 WITCH BALL
5½" Dia. 1850–1870

This is as excellent an example of marbrie, four-loop construction as you will find in Sandwich glass. Note the clear glass in one of the loops, showing that Sandwich workmanship was not up to the industry's standards for this type of glass. The original hanging wire has a wood peg fastened to the end of it. It was inserted into the opening of the ball, and positioned across the opening. Many companies made witch balls. It is extremely difficult, if not impossible, to attribute them to a particular glass house without documentation.

3229 WITCH BALL
4" Dia. 1860–1880

In addition to documentation, two clues will help attribute witch balls to Sandwich. First, there are four loops in the marbrie design. Second, to make the loop design, the threads of glass were dragged from the bottom of the ball all the way up to the top, so that the lower loops as well as the smaller loops begin and end at the opening. The opening is large enough to easily accept herbs and a wooden peg hanger. Not every marbrie ball is a witch ball. Red, white and blue ones are likely to be militia balls.

3230 WITCH BALL
4¼" Dia. 1850–1870

Witch balls of one color were hung in barns and sheds to protect animals, particularly cows. It was believed that evil spirits had the power to reduce the production of milk and could deform newborn animals. This ball was found in the cupola of a barn in East Sandwich. All Sandwich witch balls made for barn use were heavy and thick walled. Herbs could be placed inside the opening before the wood peg hanger was inserted.

3231 WITCH BALL
3" Dia. 1840–1850

This witch ball was one of four found on Cape Cod, still belonging to descendants of a Sandwich glassworker. All four have their original wood peg hangers. Each peg was hand carved and varied in diameter according to the size of the opening in the ball. A string of ribbon was tied around the notch in the peg, which was inserted into the ball. It could then be hung from a rafter.

3232 WITCH BALL
3⅛" Dia. 1840–1850

This ball has a very small opening and is very heavy. It was an extremely difficult ball to hang because the diameter of the wood peg is too narrow for the weight of the ball. It is difficult to remove an original peg released inside a ball because the ribbon or string frayed and rotted. Rather than remove the peg, other makeshift methods of hanging were devised, such as inserting a stick or a nail. This is why several hangers are occasionally found inside the ball, sometimes with their strings attached. This one has an extremely high-gloss finish. It was used in an outbuilding on Cape Cod.

3233 WITCH BALL
(a) Ball 7" Dia. 1850–1870
(b) Holder 1¾" H. x 2¾" Dia. 1835–1845

This plain witch ball was originally made for barn use. It is placed on what we now refer to as a Lacy pressed salt. Its owner has identical witch balls in blue and green, placed on identical matching blue and green Lacy holders. The Lacy pieces are well documented Sandwich patterns. The question is whether they are indeed salts, or were they made as matching stands for witch balls? We believe the Lacy holder was combined with the witch ball at a later time.

3234 MILITIA BALL (PARADE BALL)
5" Dia. 1860–1880

Glassmaking was a proud industry. In its earliest days, glassworkers set themselves apart by adopting certain customs that would differentiate them from workers in other trades. When glassworkers marched in parades, they often covered themselves with sparkling glass dust, or hung glass stars and crescents from their clothing. Sometimes they were escorted by the Militia. Each soldier carried in the muzzle of his musket a red, white and blue glass globe. Each globe had a long glass plug extension that fit into the barrel. The extension is .65 mm. or less in diameter and is the same diameter all along its length. When militia balls are found today, the plug is usually broken off, so it is incorrectly assumed that they are witch balls. Parades and ceremonies were an important part of life in the late 1800's.

3235 MILITIA BALL (PARADE BALL)
5¼" Dia. 1860–1880

Collectors of balls believe it is impossible to tell which glass company made a particular one. All of the balls in this chapter have matching dug fragments and/or family ties to Sandwich workers. A careful study of this ball shows that the workmanship at Sandwich in ornamental glass was not up to the standards set by English glass factories or by the New England Glass Company in East Cambridge, Massachusetts. This piece should not have a hanger. Small militia balls may find their way into collections of darning balls.

3236 DECORATION BALL, ALSO USED AS A HANDLED COVER BALL
6" Dia. ball with 3" L. extension 1850–1887

Decoration balls were used by the Boston and Sandwich Glass Company at trade shows. They were placed atop a wooden curb to delineate the perimeter of the booth and keep the public away from the glass-laden tables. They saw secondary use as handled cover balls for busy storekeepers, who kept pills, medicine and candy in extremely large jars. The merchant could easily grasp the tapered extension, hold the cover in one hand while he reached into the jar to dispense its contents, then replace the cover, all in one fluid motion. This practice was simply a more sophisticated application of the much earlier ball covers without handles. Unlike militia balls, these were made in single colors and the "handles" are tapered.

3237 COVER BALLS

(a) Amber 2½" Dia.
(b) Blue 3" Dia.
(c) Red 3" Dia. 1825–1850

A glass ball with the end closed was used as a cover on food containers and store jars. They are heavy because they were made to withstand rough, daily use. Flies and insects were a major problem in the 1800's. This ingenious method of protecting food was common. The balls could be tossed into a basket when they were not needed with less fear of breakage than when a cover with a finial was used, although they were weighted on the pontil end to keep them from rolling. They were gradually superseded by covers, usually with a rim and finial. Bear in mind that we are discussing tableware used in the homes of mechanics and laborers, not of the people who would have used pewter or silver on their dining table. In recent years, a decorative ball, lighter in weight, has been produced and can easily be mistaken for a Nineteenth Century cover ball. The new balls are bright and show no wear.

3238 PACKING BALLS

3" Dia. 1840–1870

When you find a free-blown ball with the end closed, and it weighs no more than a gram, it is *not* a witch ball. It is a cover to be placed on Sandwich blown vases to protect their rims during shipment. They were blown in the same color as the vase they were to be placed upon. Their primary purpose was to insure delivery of undamaged vases. Very little labor or material was invested in them.

3239 PACKING BALLS IN USE

(a) Packing Balls 2¾" Dia. 1830–1887
(b) Vase 10" H. x 3" Dia. 1840–1860

Blown vases are difficult to attribute unless they have family ties to men who worked at the factory. This vase, with its original packing ball, came from the Tobey family in Sandwich. Mrs. Tobey used the ball as a dust cover when the vase was not being used for flowers.

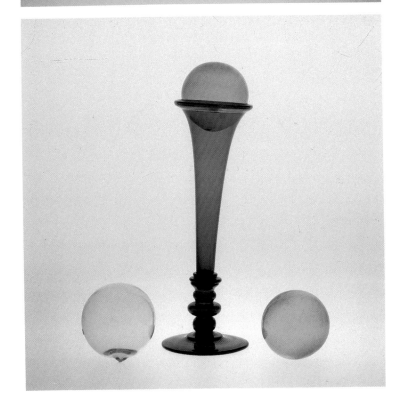

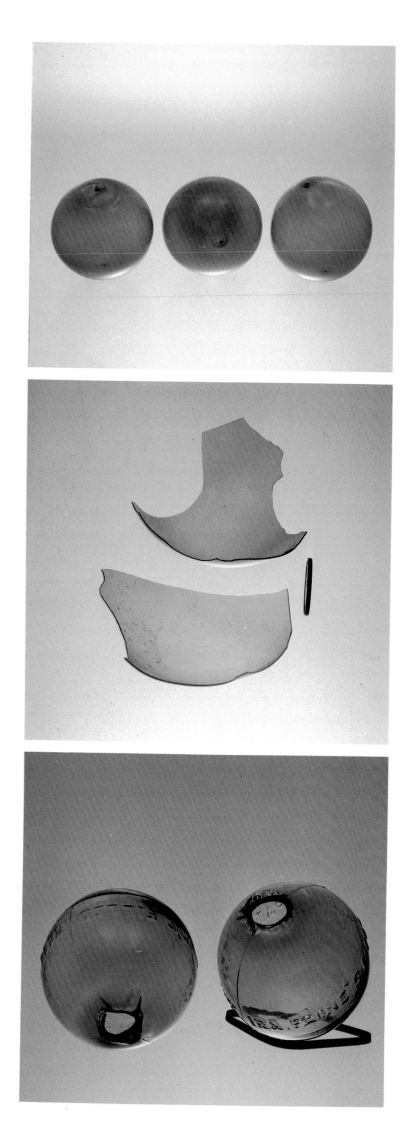

3240 PACKING BALLS
2¾" Dia. 1840–1870
These three packing balls were found at the site of the Boston and Sandwich Glass Company. They were still in position on their vases in the remains of the original shipping box. The box had been dropped and discarded. They were used, in an experimental duplication of the company's shipping methods, by Francis (Bill) Wynn of Sandwich and Ray Barlow.

3241 PACKING BALL FRAGMENTS
These fragments, dug at the Sandwich site, have a penny standing beside them to show how thin they are. Do not hold a packing ball in your hand if it is cold. The rapid temperature change will cause the air inside the ball to expand, breaking it like an eggshell.

3242 TARGET BALLS (PRACTICE BALLS)
3" Dia. 1877–1887
Target balls were filled with feathers, cotton, or confetti. They were thrown into the air for target practice in the same way that clay pigeons are used today. They are approximately the same size as packing balls, but are not free-blown. They were blown into a mold and their tops left open. This ball was patented by Ira Paine, whose name is molded into the ball around the center. It is dated October 23, 1877. Many matching fragments were dug at the Boston and Sandwich Glass Company site, although Paine's ball was also made by other glass factories from the same mold. This was a private mold that was sent to the company that quoted the lowest price.

COVERED CONTAINERS FOR SPECIALIZED USE

1830–1908

Most glass companies derived a large part of their income from the manufacture of containers that were designed for a particular use. Some had commercial use to hold hair pomade and medicinal or perfumed ointment. They were wholesaled to business firms distributing pomade or ointment or were manufactured using private molds that were owned by the distributor. Some covered pieces were not intended for commercial use and could be rightly included with pressed pattern and Lacy tableware, but their specialized use justifies their separation from those categories for detailed study. Finally, there are the one-of-a-kind patterned and figural pieces that were purchased for specialized use in the home, such as melon dishes, soap boxes, and puff jars.

The use of many of these pieces has long been open to debate, largely because some pieces made in the 1840–1870 period were designed for multiple uses. If a customer came to the Boston and Sandwich Glass Company showroom to purchase a *butter*, the salesman would likely sell him a 6" nappie (shallow bowl) with a cover. A piece listed as a *pomade* by one glass company might be listed as a

horseradish by another company. The famous figural bear produced by the Boston and Sandwich Glass Company was made for several pharmaceutical houses to hold bear grease for hair. The names of the bear grease distributors can be found molded into the bottom of the containers. But in a magazine article written by Amanda Harris in 1887, the bears are called "match safes for the five-cent stores". The bears that were sold as match holders did not have a distributor's name molded into them. However, the marked bears would also have been used for matches after the hair grease was gone.

Several footed pomade jars were manufactured in patterns that matched pressed pattern tableware. Their lower units were made in the shape of an egg cup, and a matching cover was added. Some of the lower units were the same height as an egg cup in the same pattern; others were pressed in a mold that was slightly shorter than an egg cup in the same pattern. Based on writings of glass authority Ruth Webb Lee, these pomade jars became known as "covered egg cups". Lacking documentation from an illustrated catalog, this could be a logical conclusion. However,

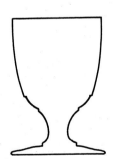

EGG CUP IF CLEAR

POMADE IF COLORED AND/OR COVERED

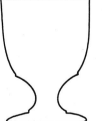

POMADE

HORSERADISH

SALT

Fig. 13   Because pressed pattern pomade and horseradish jars are not recognized as such, they have been assimilated into collections of egg cups and salts. The general proportion of most egg cups is shown in the illustration on the left. If you find a colored piece proportioned like an egg cup, you have found the lower unit of a pomade jar. The illustration in the center shows the shape most often mistaken for an egg cup. Whether clear or colored, it should have a cover and was marketed for pomade and horseradish. It is taller than a salt, shown on the right.

since we find more of them in colored opaque and translucent glass than in clear glass, this cannot be considered a justifiable conclusion today, because some of them have the same names molded into them as the figural bears. Moreover, colored glass was used to hide the color of the pomade.

We cannot find "covered egg cups" listed in bills of lading, order sheets, or catalogs from *any* glass company, either in the East or Midwest. This includes the Boston and Sandwich Glass Company, New England Glass Company, Union Glass Company, McKee and Brothers, and Bakewell, Pears and Company. Nor are "covered egg cups" mentioned in correspondence to glass factory personnel. It can be argued that, in a listing for a sugar bowl, a cover would be implied and not mentioned. Similarly, a cover for an egg cup would not be mentioned. However, careful study of factory sloar books and work sheets show that egg cups were made, *but not covers for egg cups*. So we must conclude that, after the retail customer emptied the pretty pomade jar, he very likely used the lower unit for eggs. A large family could accumulate enough pomade jars to make a set of "egg cups". Since styles did not change rapidly, the pomade distributor used the same pattern container for many years.

Unlike egg cups, covers *were* made for containers that stored condiments that were shared at the table, such as mustard and horseradish. The lower unit of a horseradish jar can also be mistaken for an egg cup or an open salt because the jar may not have an inside ridge to indicate that there should be a cover. So it becomes important to distinguish between egg cups and open salts that did not have covers, and horseradish jars that did. If the piece you are buying is an egg cup or an open salt, you are buying a complete piece. If the piece you are buying turns out to be the lower unit of a horseradish jar, you are buying only half the piece and should pay accordingly.

Conversely, if you are searching for pomades and horseradishes, you may find these jars among other types of glass utensils. If they have a stem, they may be mistakenly included in egg cup collections. If they have a short, stubby base, they could be mixed with salt collections. It is helpful to think of pomade and horseradish lower units in relation to egg cups and salts in *order of height*, as you would think of stemmed drinking vessels. When we see a champagne, we automatically think, "Goblet, champagne, wine, cordial". In the same manner, think, "Egg cup, pomade/horseradish, salt". Buy it inexpensively—then keep it in mind as you search for the cover. *The value of covered pieces is in the cover.*

An added note—a condiment container with a cover that has a cutout for a spoon handle in a *mustard*. If there is no cutout, the jar was not originally intended to be for mustard.

THESE SIMPLE HINTS WILL HELP YOU IDENTIFY SANDWICH COVERED CONTAINERS.

If you find a footed piece that is shorter than an egg cup and taller than a salt, consider the possibility that it may be the lower unit of a pomade or horseradish.

Mustards have a cutout in the cover to accept the handle of a mustard spoon.

If you find a cover that matches any of the covers in this study, buy it. The lower unit will eventually surface.

3243 LACY PEACOCK EYE (PEACOCK FEATHER) AND SHIELD RECTANGULAR DISH

(a) Dish 5⅛" H. x 6⅜" L. x 3⅞" W.

(b) Cover 2¾" H. x 5½" L. x 3⅛" W.

(c) Combined size 5⅛" H. x 6⅜" L. x 3⅞" W.

    1835–1845

All of the pieces that are designated as *Lacy* were made by pressing glass into a mold. Because pressing was a new technique that required experimentation, and because the best quality sand was not readily available to make the glass, the piece was completely covered with intricate patterns and stippling to hide defects. The double Peacock Eye on each side of the shield can be seen on other Lacy pieces. This variation of Peacock Eye has a cable pattern surrounding the "eyes" and a fine diamond pattern. The shape of the dish closely resembles covered salts made during the same period. Note the pine cone finial on the cover. *Courtesy, Sandwich Glass Museum, Sandwich Historical Society*

3244 LACY PEACOCK EYE (PEACOCK FEATHER) AND SHIELD TRAY FROM ABOVE DISH

1" H. x 8⅜" L. x 4⅝" W. 1835–1845

This tray in clear glass is the underplate for the above dish. The shields match the shield in the dish and the cover. The tray is often found in clear glass, separated from the other units. It can be identified as Sandwich by the pattern of alternating "eyes" and diamonds on the sides. There is no cable pattern surrounding the "eyes", but this combination of "eyes" and half-diamonds is repeated on the ends of the dish. A complete three-unit set is very rare. *Courtesy, Sandwich Glass Museum, Sandwich Historical Society*

3245 LACY GOTHIC ARCH AND HEART RECTANGULAR DISH WITH DOMED COVER AND TRAY

(a) Dish 2¾" H. x 6¼" L. x 4" W.
(b) Cover 2⅜" H. x 5⅞" L. x 3⅜" W.
(c) Tray 1" H. x 7¼" L. x 4½" W.
(d) Combined size 5⅜" H. x 7¼" L. x 4½" W.
    1835–1845

Many seemingly unrelated patterns were combined on Lacy pieces. On three-unit combinations, not every pattern appears on each of the units. There are gothic arches and hearts on the sides of the dish. The arches are repeated on the cover, but the hearts are not. The hearts are repeated on the tray, but the arches are not. This set is very seldom found complete. Watch for the units separately, in clear and color. They will often be in box lots at auctions. *Courtesy, Sandwich Glass Museum, Sandwich Historical Society*

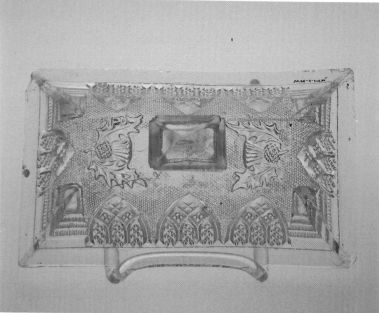

3246 LACY GOTHIC ARCH DOMED COVER FROM ABOVE DISH

Note the pattern of thistles on the cover—completely foreign to the dish itself. The pattern is on the inside of the cover, but on the outside of the dish. The value of rare covered pieces is in the cover. If you see a cover for sale, don't pass it up. The lower unit will eventually be found.

3247 LACY GOTHIC ARCH AND HEART RECTANGULAR DISH WITH STEPPED COVER AND TRAY

(a) Dish 2¾" H. x 6¼" L. x 4" W.
(b) Cover 2½" H. x 5¾" L. x 3⅜" W.
(c) Tray 1" H. x 7¼" L. x 4½" W.
(d) Combined size 5⅜" H. x 7¼" L. x 4½" W.
    1835–1845

This three-piece assembly has the same dish and tray, but the cover is completely different. The cover is stepped instead of domed. The arches on the cover were lengthened to cover the top of the step. This gives the complete set a different look. The tray with its Heart border is shown on the following page. *Courtesy, Sandwich Glass Museum, Sandwich Historical Society*

3248 LACY GOTHIC ARCH STEPPED COVER FROM ABOVE DISH

Compare this stepped cover to the domed cover. Instead of thistles, there are two quatrefoils on each side of the finial. The Toledo Museum of Art has a beautiful deep blue complete set in their collection. The pattern on the cover of the Toledo piece can barely be seen because it is on the inside. It may have been easier to make the mold for the cover with the pattern on the inside, but our photo of this piece in color would not have shown the detail of the pattern.

3249 LACY HEART TRAY FROM GOTHIC ARCH AND HEART DISH

1⅛" H. x 7" L. x 4⅝" W. 1835-1845

The only resemblance to the dish is the pattern of hearts and the scallop and point rim that matches the rim of the dish. Note the tiny flowers in the center, a pattern used on toy dishes. Fragments also show this tray with a waffle center. Another variation has the *U.S.F. Constitution* in the center. The *Constitution* tray is a rare historical piece and very likely was not meant to be used with the dish and cover. Trays that match Lacy rectangular dishes have a scallop and point rim. *Courtesy, Sandwich Glass Museum, Sandwich Historical Society*

3250 PRESSED HORN OF PLENTY (COMET) RECTANGULAR DISH

(a) Dish 2⅞" H. x 6½" L. x 4" W.
(b) Cover 2¾" H. x 5⅞" L. x 3⅜" W.
(c) Combined size 5¼" H. x 6½" L. x 4" W.
   1845-1855

The pattern, called *Horn of Plenty* today, was called *Comet* by the factories that made it. It was made over a long period of time, but the shape of this piece indicates early vintage. Rectangular covered dishes were not practical because the corners of the cover struck the rim of the dish, easily damaging both. Therefore, this form was discontinued early. Although the pattern is a carry-over from the Lacy Period, the background is not stippled. With the beginning of complete lines of pressed pattern tableware, all of the elements that make up the pattern are on both units. If a rectangular tray was part of the set, the Comet pattern should be on the rim. *Courtesy, Sandwich Glass Museum, Sandwich Historical Society*

3251 BLOWN MOLDED SANDWICH MELON DISH

(a) Dish 2⅝" H. x 5⅜" L. x 4" W.
(b) Cover 3⅛" H. x 5½" L. x 4" W.
(c) Pressed underplate 1⅛" H. x 7⅜" L. x 6" W.
(d) Combined size 5⅞" H. x 7⅜" L. x 6" W.
    1850–1870

The Sandwich Melon is one of the rarest pieces manufactured by the Boston and Sandwich Glass Company. We believe it was made in other colors. The stem finial can be seen on other pieces made in Sandwich, such as the Overshot covered bowl shown on page 121 in Volume 4. One of the ways to identify an original Sandwich melon is to look inside the cover, and you will see a rough pontil mark under the stem finial. According to the Sandwich Glass Museum, there are only two known examples of this truly unique dish and underplate. *Courtesy, Sandwich Glass Museum, Sandwich Historical Society*

3252 UNITS OF ABOVE DISH

The melon is split horizontally in the center, and the cover will go on only one way. The cover has nine ribs, and no rim. The bottom of the melon has eleven ribs, and a rim over which the cover fits. The underplate was pressed into the form of a melon leaf with an irregular outer edge. It also has a stem, and a center deep enough to accept the base of the melon.

3253 PRESSED HEN DISH

(a) Dish 1⅞" H. x 7⅜" L. x 5¼" W.
(b) Cover 4" H. x 8" L. x 5¾" W.
(c) Combined size 5¾" H. x 8" L. x 5¾" W.
    1850–1870

The construction of the Sandwich hen is unique in several ways. The cover consists of the hen sitting in the center surrounded by a wide rim of straw. The side of the oval dish has a drape pattern that alternates with two vertical lines, while the base has a completely unrelated block pattern. Neither pattern relates to the hen. It is difficult to find the hen without damage to the beak and comb. We have seen this piece in clear, canary, green, and several shades of blue. If each unit is a different color, use caution—the units may be married.

3254 UNITS OF ABOVE HEN DISH

This photo shows the unusual turn of the hen's head. The tail is hollow, with the opening beneath the cover. Some hens made in the Pittsburgh area have hollow tails that open to the back of the tail. Note the pattern on the oval dish. If found alone at an antiques show, it could easily be overlooked or thought to be French.

3255 PRESSED SPANIEL DISH

(a) Dish 1⅞" H. x 4⅝" L. x 3¼" W.
(b) Cover 2¼" H. x 4¼" L. x 2¾" W.
(c) Combined size 3⅜" H. x 4⅝" L. x 3¼" W.
   1895–1908

Ruth Webb Lee, in her book *Victorian Glass*, states that the dog can positively be attributed to Sandwich. Other authorities believe the green cast to the glass make it an unlikely candidate for Boston and Sandwich Glass Company manufacture. Actually, the spaniel, with this base, was probably made by one of the short-lived companies that attempted production at the Boston and Sandwich site. This accounts for the scarcity of the spaniel. Some fragments were found at the site, but very few, indicating an extremely short production period. A 1906 newspaper reported that the Sandwich Glass Company was making novelties. The Alton Manufacturing Company also produced small amounts of novelties until 1908. The lattice pattern is only on the two long sides. The ends are stippled and the rim is beaded. An oval dish with a similar spaniel was made by McKee. The Sandwich dish is rectangular.

3256 PRESSED TURTLE SOAP DISH

(a) Base 1¼" H. x 5¼" L. x 2¾" W.
(b) Shell cover 1" H. x 4⅜" L. x 3¼" W.
(c) Combined size 2¼" H. x 5⅜" L. x 3¼" W.
   1907–1908

The turtle's shell is the cover of the soap dish. The deep grooves separating the segments of the shell are gilded. There are no shell markings under the bottom unit. The mouth and eyes are very distinct. A mold mark can be seen running down the center of the head, between the eyes, bisecting the mouth, and continuing down the center of the neck to the base. This was a product of the Alton Manufacturing Company. It can be found in opaque white without the gilding and brown color. *Courtesy, Sandwich Glass Museum, Sandwich Historical Society*

3257 PRESSED HORSESHOE BOX

1¾" H. x 3½" L. x 3⅛" W. 1907–1908

This masculine box was made to hold collar buttons and similar accessories on a man's chest-of-drawers. The head of a horse is on the cover, surrounded by a horseshoe. Two horseshoes are molded into the end panel. A whip and bugle can be seen on each side. *Courtesy, Sandwich Glass Museum, Sandwich Historical Society*

3258 PRESSED HORSESHOE BOX
1½" H. x 3½" L. x 3" W. May 1907

Here is absolute proof of Sandwich manufacture—the same box as shown above, signed and dated by the Alton Manufacturing Company. It is easy to differentiate between pieces decorated by the original Boston and Sandwich Glass Company and pieces inexpensively decorated by the several companies that later occupied the same buildings. Study this piece and the pressed turtle soap dish and the pressed Great Blue Heron vase attributed to the Alton Manufacturing Company in Chapter 2. You will find that the high standards set by the Boston and Sandwich Glass Company were not maintained by those who attempted to re-open the factory. *Courtesy, Sandwich Glass Museum, Sandwich Historical Society*

3259 PRESSED DRUM POMADE
3¾" H. x 2½" Dia. 1850-1870

This is the only figural drum known to have been manufactured in Sandwich. It was made in two sizes, the tall one shown here and a shorter one that is 2½" high. The cover is nothing more than a thin disk that rests on a recessed ridge. The drumstick, intended to be used as a hand hold, protrudes only ³⁄₁₆" above the rim of the drum, so it is virtually impossible to remove the cover without turning the drum over and dropping the cover in your hand. As a result of this design, the covers were easily broken. A shield can be seen lying on its side under the ropes of the drum. An amethyst drum in our collection is marked "PHALON & SON" on the shield. The blue drum in this photo is not marked. It may have had a paper label. Other companies made smaller drums as parts of a child's set of tableware and large ones for an adult-size set. Made primarily in clear glass, they do not have the shield.

3260 PRESSED CAVALIER POMADE
3¾" H. 1850-1870

This gay, sprightly fellow is unique to Sandwich. His sitting position allows the jar to hold the same amount of pomade as the same size bear would hold and gives stability. The ones we have examined are marked "E. T. S. & Co NY." underneath. Two types of hats were made: the short plumed one shown here, fragments of which were dug at the Boston and Sandwich site, and a tall top hat patterned after the Prism Panel toy tumbler made by the Cape Cod Glass Company and shown in Chapter 10. A photo of the tall version can be seen in the booklet *Sandwich Glass*, published by the Sandwich Historical Society. *The brim of the hat is part of the lower unit.* The crown and plume form the cover, and must match in color. If the cover is a different color or a different shade, the units are married and the value is significantly decreased.

3261 PRESSED BEAR JARS

(a) Large, "R. & G. A. WRIGHT" on base 5⅛" H.

(b) Medium, "J. HAUEL & CO. PHILADA." on base 4½" H.

(c) Small, no mark on base 3¾" H. 1850–1887

Figural bears were originally designed to hold bear grease which, according to a label at the Sandwich Glass Museum, was for "promoting the growth and luxuriance of hair". As the bear population decreased, an odorless pomade took the place of the grease. Bear A is the largest size normally found, but the rarest was at least 8" high and held a quart or more. It was sometimes placed at the back of the kitchen stove and used as a receptacle for waste fat. The names on the base are those of the retail distributors of the contents. Other bears are marked "X BAZIN PHILA", "PHALON & SON NY", "F. B. STROUSE NY", and "EUGENE BIZE & FRICKE SUCCESSOR TO J. HAUEL & C". A narrow paper label surrounded the neck sealing the head to the body. Some bears are not marked and were sold by the Boston and Sandwich Glass Company directly to the retail customer to be used as match boxes.

3262 PRESSED BEAR JARS

(a) Clambroth

(b) Black amethyst fragment

(c) Black amethyst

(d) Opaque white 3¾" H. 1850–1887

These are the smallest size. The black amethyst was made over a long period of time and is the most common. It was listed in 1883 union records, but no other color was given as a regular line item. In order of scarcity, clambroth is second, followed by white and blue. Diggings at the factory show colors that have never been found — opaque green, opaque lilac, and soft pink. The color we call *clambroth* was known as *alabaster*.

3263 PRESSED BEAR JAR

(a) Blue, "X BAZIN PHILADA" on base 4⅝" H.

(b) Wooden bear contemporary to above 4⅞" H. 1850–1870

Xavier Bazin founded his perfumery and toilet soap laboratory in 1850. This style of bear is very difficult to find. He sits back on his haunches, his front paws are crossed, and there is a chain around his neck. He does not have a muzzle. The bear on the right is made of wood and is almost identical except for the collar around his neck. The more common glass bear was also made in pottery and has an English registry mark. This raises the eternal question — which one is a copy? The answer — probably neither. The bear was a piece that took the buying public's fancy and was manufactured by several different companies in several mediums. In the same way, Tulip vases were made in both glass and pottery, while Lacy glass pieces were duplicated in Meissen porcelain.

3264 PRESSED WOLF JAR COVER
1¼" H. 1850–1870

The wolf head has been dug in sufficient quantities to establish its origin as the Boston and Sandwich Glass Company, but we have found neither the body alone nor a complete jar. The wolf can be differentiated from the bear by examining the ears. They are hollowed out and are positioned differently. The eyes are lower, slanted, and not as widely opened. The snout is shorter and is not muzzled. We have seen the wolf head used with a bear body, but we do not believe the jar was shipped from the factory this way.

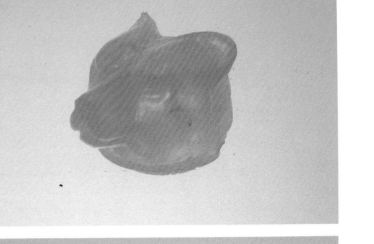

3265 PRESSED CABLE POMADE
5" H. x 2⅝" Dia. 1840–1870

The bottom unit of this pomade was marketed as the egg cup in Cable pressed pattern tableware. Adding a cover turned it into a pomade, so the Boston and Sandwich Glass Company used the same mold for several purposes. This piece has also been found in opaque green. Most of the pieces originally designed for pomade have a small unpatterned area where a tiny paper label was applied—such as the panel between the Cable pattern, the "eye" in Bull's Eye and Bar, and the band above Diamond Point. In clear glass, this covered piece could also be used for horseradish. *Courtesy, Sandwich Glass Museum, Sandwich Historical Society*

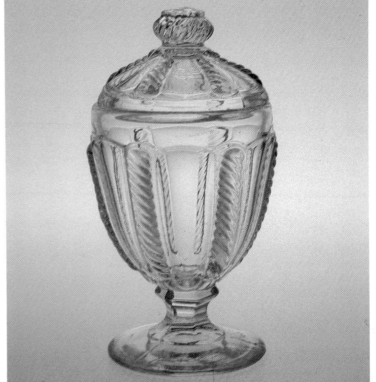

3266 PRESSED FLAT DIAMOND AND PANEL POMADE
6⅝" H. X 2½" Dia. 1850–1870

Pomade was a perfumed ointment, used primarily for the hair. Sometimes an egg cup mold was used to make the bottom unit of the pomade. Many collectors, therefore, mistakenly believe that these pomade jars are covered egg cups, but that was not the intent. Most pomades that are egg cup-shaped were produced in translucent and opaque colors because the color of the ointment was not attractive. This pomade is taller than most, but the height is in the cover. The cover appears to be darker than the bottom unit, which could suggest that the cover was replaced. However, the cover is darker only because it is thicker. When considering a purchase, hold each unit up to a bright light and look through the glass. If each unit is a different *hue*, they were combined at a later time. *Courtesy of The Toledo Museum of Art (Acc. No. 65.16)*

3268 PRESSED BULL'S EYE (LAWRENCE) POMADES

(a) Complete with cover 5⅜" H. x 2⅝" Dia.
(b) Lower unit only 3⅞" H. x 2⅝" Dia. 1850–1870
Our acquisition of the Wennerstrom fragment collection resulted in a wealth of new information. Frank and June Wennerstrom dug only at the site of the Cape Cod Glass Works, so the collection is not contaminated by fragments from the Boston and Sandwich Glass Company site. Fragments of this pomade were found in the Wennerstrom diggings, so the piece can be attributed to the Cape Cod Glass Works and the Cape Cod Glass Company, as well as to the Boston and Sandwich Glass Company. It was made in several other translucent pastel colors. The formulas for these colors are in James D. Lloyd's formula book, written in 1868, when Lloyd was working at the Cape Cod Glass Company. Full sets of tableware were made in this pattern, which can be seen in a New England Glass Company catalog. The original pattern name was *Lawrence. The Bennington Museum, Bennington, Vermont*

3267 PRESSED BULL'S EYE AND BAR

(a) Wooden pattern
(b) Pressed pomade 1850–1870
Before a mold was made, the pattern was first carved in wood. The wooden pattern shown here is the bottom part of the pomade. Pomades were shipped out of the factory to wholesale houses that filled them with the ointment. In most cases, after the container was empty, the bottom unit was used for an egg cup. We cannot find in the records of any glass company an indication that *covered* egg cups were sold as part of a tableware pattern. We suggest that you not buy a *colored* jar, hoping to locate a matching cover, unless it is reasonably priced. It is virtually impossible to find one made from the same batch of glass, so the color will not be an exact match. *Courtesy, Sandwich Glass Museum, Sandwich Historical Society*

3269 PRESSED DIAMOND POINT (SHARP DIAMOND) POMADE

5⅜" H. x 2⅝" Dia. 1850–1870
This pattern was made under the name *Sharp Diamond*. The bottom unit was pressed in a mold that was more complicated than most. Four seams run vertically through the diamond pattern, but only two opposite ones continue straight down the stem and across the foot. The other two make a right angle below the pattern, then angle again to continued down the stem. We have no idea why the pattern could not have been made in a mold with the usual three seams, as was done for the cover. Note the protrusion below the diamonds that makes up the upper part of the stem. It is not on the mold used to make the Diamond Point egg cup. The pomade's close resemblance to the egg cup made it an excellent substitute. Note the discoloration along the mold mark. Pieces in this clambroth (alabaster) color often have black spots. While we wish they were not present, they do not detract from value.

3270 PRESSED FINE RIB (REEDED) WITH SHIELD POMADE
5½" H. x 2⅝" Dia. 1850–1870
Fine Rib tableware pieces were made by several factories in New England and Pennsylvania. The catalog name was *Reeded*. The pomade is attributed to Sandwich. Only the pomade always has a shield. The shield may have the name of the distributor molded into it, such as "Phalon & Son". Some shields are smooth to take a paper label. The pomades were made in several colors and also in clear. If you find a Fine Rib pomade without the shield, you have two married pieces—a pomade cover on an egg cup.

3271 PRESSED FINE RIB (REEDED)
(a) Pomade, with shield 3½" H. x 2⅝" Dia.
(b) Egg cup, no shield 4" H. x 2⅝" Dia. 1850–1870
Dug fragments show that both pieces were made by the Boston and Sandwich Glass Company. There can be no argument about the difference when they are placed side by side. Note the height of the egg cup. It is approximately the size of most egg cups made during this time period. The green pomade is shorter than the egg cup, but taller than a salt. The pomade was made in a three-piece mold, the egg cup in a two-piece mold. This can be seen by holding each one up to the light and looking down from the top onto the upper surface of the foot. The pomade has three mold marks that extend to the outer edge of the foot, which was not reworked after removal from the mold. The foot of the egg cup has the remains of two mold marks near the stem. The foot was expanded and fire polished, obliterating the marks. The lack of finish work on the pomade is another indication that it was meant for one-time use as a container for a commercial product.

3272 PRESSED NEW YORK HONEYCOMB (NEW YORK, UTICA) POMADE
4¼" H. x 2½" Dia., without cover 1850–1870
At the time this pomade jar was made, the term *Honeycomb* was not used. Pieces with the pattern half way up the sides were called *New York* by the New England Glass Company and *New York Honeycomb* by collectors. The pattern is illustrated in the Cape Cod Glass Company list of glassware, reprinted in Chapter 4 of this book, where it is called *Utica*. Large quantities of fragments were found at the Boston and Sandwich Glass Company site, and it was made by many other factories as well. In her book *Glass Tableware, Bowls & Vases*, Jane S. Spillman notes that this shape is confusing because it is large for an egg cup, but has a stem too short for a wine. It is neither an egg cup nor a wine, but is the lower unit of a pomade jar. We have seen it with the pomade distributor's name molded into the upper surface of the base in a circle. To be complete, it must have a matching cover.

3273 PRESSED VERNON HONEYCOMB (VERNON) POMADE

4¾" H. x 2¼" Dia. 1850–1870

The present-day collector calls this pattern *Honeycomb*, sometimes preceded by the original name of the pattern—in this instance, *Vernon*. On Vernon pieces, the honeycomb pattern extends almost to the rim of the lower unit. Fragments show that it was made in quantity at the Boston and Sandwich Glass Company. This piece is also illustrated in a New England Glass Company catalog, where it is listed as a pomade. It is shown in the New England catalog with a complete line of Vernon tableware, so it may not have been a commercial piece. Except for the octagonal finial and the ten-sided short stem, it is a miniature version of the Vernon sugar bowl. A different mold was used for Vernon egg cups. An 1861 catalog from James B. Lyon and Company, a Pittsburgh manufacturer, shows a similar piece in Cincinnati, the pattern name for another Honeycomb variant. It is listed as a horseradish.

3274 PRESSED GIANT HONEYCOMB HORSERADISH

4¾" H. x 2¾" Dia. 1845–1860

This is a variant of the Honeycomb pattern made by several companies in both New England and Pittsburgh. The pattern is so large that three rows complete the lower unit from the scallops on the rim to the scallops on the base. Two rows of pattern are on the cover. The finial is a common one found on other Sandwich items. Note again the proportions of the lower unit. Careful study of factory catalogs reveals that horseradish containers were made in a number of patterns. However, they are largely ignored as such by collectors because they are bought without their covers. If they have a stem, they find their way into egg cup collections. If they have a short stubby base, they are included in salt collections. *Courtesy, Sandwich Glass Museum, Sandwich Historical Society*

3275 PRESSED SAWTOOTH (MITRE DIAMOND) POMADE

3" H. x 2¾" Dia. 1850–1870

Because of an early lack of original documentation, this pattern became known as *Sawtooth*. A New England Glass Company catalog lists it as *Mitre Diamond*, and pieces by that name can be found on Boston and Sandwich Glass Company invoices. Several Midwest factories produced it also, so there are many variants that differ only slightly from one another. This Sandwich pomade has a cover that one usually associates with spice jars and wide-mouthed apothecary jars. Even though the cover is hollow with a rayed pattern beneath the finial, the pomade was called *stoppered* because the cover was ground to fit the inside of the jar in the same manner as the plug of a stopper. This mold was also used to make an oil bottle by drawing the top of the jar into a long neck, then forming a spout and applying a handle. *Courtesy, Sandwich Glass Museum, Sandwich Historical Society*

3276 PRESSED SAWTOOTH (MITRE DIAMOND) HORSERADISH OR SALT

(a) Small finial, ridged foot 5⅜" H. x 2½" Dia.
(b) Faceted finial, smooth base 5¼" H. x 2¼" Dia.
1850–1870

This container is more easily found than any other. Note the variations in the finial and foot. Fragments of all four units were dug in quantity at the Boston and Sandwich site, and they are interchangeable. A canary one in our collection has the ridged foot on A and the faceted finial of B. Usually considered to be a salt, it may originally have been designed for horseradish. The mold's versatility resulted in additional use when it was made in non-lead glass at a later time by Bryce Brothers of Pittsburgh. They manufactured a toy tableware set and used this piece as the sugar. The cover of the toy sugar has the small finial.

3277 PRESSED SAWTOOTH (MITRE DIAMOND)

(a) Wooden pattern for cover with faceted finial
(b) Pressed horseradish or salt

The wooden pattern was the first step in making the mold for the cover. In this photo, it has been placed on an opal lower unit to show how the diamonds interlock, obviating the need for an inner rim. The diamonds increase in size from the finial to the rim, then decrease in size from the rim to the hexagonal stem. There are the same number of diamonds in each horizontal row. Not all pieces of Mitre Diamond have a sawtooth edge. Most pieces do, but an open salt has a plain rim. Note the plain foot on this variant. *Courtesy, Sandwich Glass Museum, Sandwich Historical Society*

3278 LACY PEACOCK EYE (PEACOCK FEATHER) MUSTARD

2½" H. x 2¾" Dia. 1830–1845

Without its cover, this piece could be mistaken by a novice collector for a child's mug. It is often shown with an underplate, but there is nothing in the records to prove that an underplate is correct. The underplates we have studied do not fit the base of the container. The pattern more closely resembles peacock feathers than a peacock's eye, but we will not change the name established by Ruth Webb Lee. The pattern is on the outside of the container, but is on the inside of the cover. This was common at Sandwich and works well with clear glass. When this mustard was made in a deep color, the pattern cannot be seen through the cover. The cover is cut out to accept a mustard spoon, which was usually made of bone or olive wood. The handle was molded as part of the container. Note the fine diamond point pattern alternating with stippling, one of many variations of the Peacock Eye pattern. *Courtesy of The Toledo Museum of Art (Acc. No. 68.20)*

3279 PRESSED OPAL LUNCH CASTER
(a) Complete caster 5¼" H.; 4⅜" across
(b) Mustard cover 1½" H. x 2⅛" Dia. 1870–1887
We have shown you a very early mustard and now a very late one. During the middle years, a mustard bottle was included in four and five-bottle caster sets and very few individual ones were made. Containers that were designed for mustard always have a cutout in the cover for the spoon. This piece is pictured in the 1874 Boston and Sandwich Glass Company catalog and belonged to the family of glassworker Joseph Henry Lapham. Note the detail on the finial of the cover. The pattern of ribs is similar to the blown molded cologne in Chapter 5. If you find this set without its cover, you only have half of the piece. The plain rim on the mustard compartment would make the lack of a cover obvious. *Courtesy, Sandwich Glass Museum, Sandwich Historical Society*

3280 PRESSED COVERED BASKETS
(a) Match holder 4¾" H. x 2¾" Dia.
(b) Toothpick holder 4" H. x 2½" Dia. 1850–1870
This matched set of baskets still had their original contents when we photographed them in the home of descendants of Sandwich glassworkers. Basket A held long matches that had to be struck on a flint. Basket B held the first of the wooden toothpicks. The knopped finial made the cover easy to grasp and simple to remove without chipping or breaking. They are, in the opinion of the authors, examples of Sandwich at its finest. Note the handles on the side of the baskets. Study the weave of the basket—three horizontal rods woven over and under a single vertical rod. The difference between the Sandwich weave and a similar weave made in Baccarat, France, is shown in the illustration.

3281 PRESSED COVERED BASKETS
(a) Bottom unit of match holder
(b) Complete toothpick holder
The bottom unit of the match holder and toothpick holder has a plain rim above the weave pattern. A flange on the cover fits inside the rim. If you buy a Sandwich basket with a plain rim, remember that you are buying only half the piece. The bottom unit alone is worth less than half the value of the complete covered piece. The canary and green covers without their finials were dug at the Boston and Sandwich Glass Company site.

3282 PRESSED BASKETS
(a) 1½" H.
(b) 2" H. 1850-1870

Here are Sandwich baskets with the same weave pattern, but they were not designed to have covers. The rims are patterned as they would have been finished on real Nineteenth Century woven wicker baskets. Note that basket B is approximately the same size as the bottom unit of the covered basket match holder, shown in photo 3281. There can be handles on the sides. If you find a Sandwich basket with the patterned rim, you have a complete piece. Its value is greater than the value of the bottom unit alone of the covered basket. Several Pennsylvania glass factories produced figural basket items during the 1870's and 1880's. The Pennsylvania patterns do not stand out in deep relief and the glass is of lesser quality. We are grateful for the help of the Sandwich glassmakers' descendants who have so willingly allowed us to photograph their heirlooms.

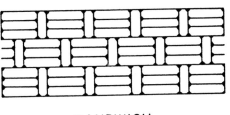

SANDWICH

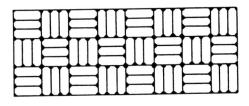

BACCARAT

Fig. 14 The basket pattern used on Sandwich toothpick holders and match holders is a wicker weave composed of three pliable horizontal rods woven over and under widely spaced, single, rigid vertical rods. The Baccarat weave of three horizontal rods woven over and under three closely spaced vertical rods gives the effect of a splint basket.

Fig. 15 **BASKET PATTERN ON OVAL COVER FRAGMENT** 5" L. x 3" W. approximate size of cover 1850-1870

Fragments of this basket pattern were dug in Sandwich. The largest fragment we have seen is on display at the Sandwich Glass Museum. It is a piece of a translucent blue oval cover, the type that could have been used on a large oval top hat. Many covered hats were made by Compagnie des Cristalleries de Baccarat, but they have the weave pattern of three vertical rods shown previously. To date, we have not located a complete cover with its bottom unit.

3283 PRESSED DENTIFRICE JAR
3½" H. with metal cover; 2" Dia. 1840-1860

Although our forefathers might not have admonished their children to brush their teeth three times a day, tooth powder and toothbrushes were a part of their toilet. The *Yarmouth Register*, a Cape Cod newspaper, advertised domestic and British tooth powder, compound chlorine tooth wash, and toothbrushes as early as 1837. This jar held tooth powder. A small amount of the powder was coaxed into the bowl-shaped metal cover and mixed with water to form a paste. The jar, metal cover, and melted fragments were dug at the Boston and Sandwich site.

3284 PRESSED DENTIFRICE JAR

3⅛" H. x 2¾" Dia. 1840–1860

This jar was manufactured by the Boston and Sandwich Glass Company and was wholesaled to the company that made the tooth powder. The piece is octagonal, with an oval in each of the eight panels. There is no pattern on the octagonal cover. It is perfectly flat so that a paper label could be pasted on it. A similar jar was made in France in the 1840's. The French jar is hexagonal and its six panels extend to a ridge just below the rim. *The Bennington Museum, Bennington, Vermont*

3285 PRESSED ACORN WITH BEADING SOAP BOX

(a) Box 2½" H. x 3½" Dia.
(b) Cover 1" H. x 3¾" Dia.
(c) Combined size 3½" H. x 3¾" Dia. 1850–1870

Many fragments of this box have been recovered from the Boston and Sandwich Glass Company site, in a variety of colors. The use of this piece was determined from a description of a like item illustrated in a French catalog. The acorns and oak leaves on the box and cover are in deep relief not often associated with American pressed glass. The bottom is stippled, and there is stippling on the surface where there is no design. The cover fits snugly.

3286 UNITS OF ABOVE SOAP BOX

The dug fragments were found in the portion of the dump known to have been used in 1850. The Sandwich Glass Museum has a canary soap box on display. A reproduction was made by the Wheaton Glass Company. It is the same diameter, but is shorter and there is no stippling. The reproduction is signed.

3287 BLOWN MOLDED ROSETTE PUFF BOX
(a) Box (Jar) 2⅝" H. x 4⅛" Dia.
(b) Pressed Cover 1" H. x 4⅛" Dia.
(c) Combined size 3⅜" H. x 4⅛" Dia. 1850–1870
Today we would call this piece a *powder jar*. It originally
held a puff used to powder hair. The six-petaled rosettes
at the base of the jar are considerably smaller than the
ones near the top. Six rows of evenly spaced rosettes make
up the jar, which was blown into a mold and weighs less
than half the weight of the cover. The cover is thick and
heavy because it was pressed into a mold. *Courtesy, Sandwich Glass Museum, Sandwich Historical Society*

3288 UNITS OF ABOVE PUFF BOX
The cover has a rim, which fits inside the box. A single
row of rosettes surrounds the large dahlia-like rosette that
makes up the center. The cover does not have a finial,
making the box difficult to open. In order to open it, one
must grasp the whole cover.

3289 PRESSED OVAL HOBNAIL PUFF BOX
(a) Box 3¼" H. x 4½" Dia.
(b) Cover 3" H. x 3½" Dia.
(c) Combined size 5¾" H. x 4½" Dia. 1850–1870
This puff box was made to be combined with a pair of the
Oval Hobnail colognes shown in the cologne chapter. It
was also made in France. The Sandwich one can be identified by looking inside the cover. A heavy, rough pontil
mark is directly under the finial, where the cover was held
while the finial was reheated and bent. The French box
is lighter in weight, and the underside of the cover is
smoothly molded. This stem finial was also used on the
melon dish. The number of dug fragments indicate that
it was made in many colors.

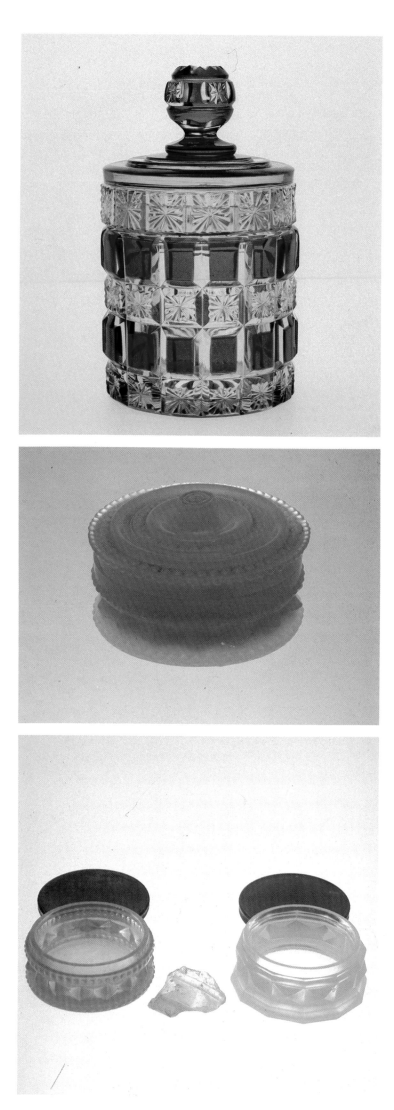

3290 CUT OVERLAY PANEL AND STAR PUFF BOX

(a) Box 3" H. x 2⅞" Dia.
(b) Cover 2¼" H. x 2⅞" Dia.
(c) Combined size 4¾" H. x 2⅞" Dia. 1850–1870

This puff box was blown into a mold and then cut to match the Panel and Star cologne. Concentric rings on the cover match rings on the shoulder of the cologne. This piece was difficult to use without damaging it. The upper row of stars is on the side of the cover, not the jar. The cover must be removed by lifting it vertically. Otherwise, the rim of the cover will catch the inner rim of the jar and chip it. Like a stopper, the cover is fitted to this particular jar. There is a number inscribed inside the cover, beneath the finial. It matches the number on the base of the jar. A star is cut into the top of the finial. The base also has a star.

3291 PRESSED MITRE DIAMOND WITH BEADING OINTMENT BOX

1½" H. x 2¾" Dia. 1840–1845

These small containers held salves that were the consistency of vaseline. The earliest of them had glass covers. There are two rings of beads on the upper surface of the cover, alternating with plain concentric rings. Concentric rings are repeated on the finial. A third ring of beads surrounds the cover, just underneath the very edge. The height of this box indicates large capacity, but the base is ½" thick and is only slightly recessed. When emptied, this piece may have seen double duty as a patch box.

3292 PRESSED OINTMENT BOXES

(a) Mitre Diamond with Beading
(b) Diamond Panel 1⅛" H. x 2¾" Dia. 1840–1860

Each of the ointment boxes shown here matches fragments dug in quantity at the Boston and Sandwich Glass Company site, but they were not produced exclusively at Sandwich. They were also produced by the New England Glass Company, so they are not difficult to find. Ointments were applied topically to burns and skin disorders. Before Federal control of food and drug advertising, a purchased remedy was expected to cure everything. Box A has the same pattern as the box with the glass cover. It is not as high, but holds the same amount. It has a thin base, so the rim begins just above the beading. It holds the same amount of ointment as a box with a thicker base, but many more could be made from the same amount of glass. Box B has a raised diamond in each of twelve panels.

3293 PRESSED OINTMENT BOXES
(a) Outlined Diamond with Beading 1" H. x 2⅝" Dia.
(b) Concave Panels, standing on its side 1⅛" H. x
    2¾" Dia. 1840–1860

Ointment boxes were made in clear glass as well as fiery opalescent. There are degrees of opalescence. Some boxes barely have color, and others that are very fiery have bases that are almost transparent. Covers in good condition are difficult to locate because the salve ate into the soft metal and dissolved it. Note how shallow the boxes are compared to the penny in the foreground.

3294 PRESSED OINTMENT BOXES
(a) Concave Panels 1⅛" H. x 2¾" Dia.
(b) Diamond, Fleur-de-lis and Oval in Panels
    1⅛" H. x 2⅝" Dia. 1840–1860

Some covers are pewter, some are white metal, and some are tin. They do not fit tightly. The boxes could be turned upside down without spilling the contents. We have seen an ointment box with an original paper label affixed to the top of the cover, but the words were illegible. Box A has twelve concave panels. A blue box in our collection has straight sides with sixteen panels. The base is marked "DR. L. C. DALE'S PATENT 1850". Box B has nine panels, with each motif repeated three times.

3295 PRESSED OINTMENT BOX
1⅜" H. x 2" Dia. 1850–1873

Inexpensive commercial containers were made by many glass factories, including the Boston and Sandwich Glass Company. Inside the cover is the mark "J. P. PRAY'S ROSALINE NEW YORK". *Rosaline* was a face cream or ointment made from crushed rose hips. The recessed base is marked "½ oz". This indicates the capacity of the box, not necessarily the weight of the contents. The same box without the lettering inside the cover might contain patches, which weighed practically nothing. This piece is fiery opalescent, which helps us to date it. It, and many like it, were dug at the factory site. The 1887 sloar book notes that Edward Brady's shop made 498 ¾ oz. rosaline boxes for Pray the week of August 1.

3296 PRESSED OPAL POMADE BOXES
(a) Large 1¼" H. x 2½" Dia.
(b) Small 1⅛" H. x 1¾" Dia. 1873–1887

A list of pressed ware recorded by Sandwich union members in 1883 includes two-ounce pomades. A trade catalog from a Pittsburgh firm indicates that these small round containers were also sold as patch boxes. The tiny silk patches were used by Nineteenth Century women as "beauty spots" to hide defects and smallpox scars. These boxes were dug at the Boston and Sandwich Glass Company site. The glass is poor quality because they were made for one-time use only. A circle about the size of a penny is in the inside center of the cover and base of the larger box. Numbers or letters molded into the recessed base do not always indicate capacity. The smaller box is marked "700¼". The style or stock number is 700 and the capacity is ¼ ounce. If there were several identical molds for the same container, a small letter or number identified each mold in case there was a problem in the pressing. Box A is marked "2" on the base and box B is marked "C".

3297 PRESSED OPAL PATCH BOX
DECORATED WITH LADY TRANSFER PRINT
1½" H. x 3¼" Dia. 1873–1887

This 1½ ounce patch box was meant to be used on a dressing table. To make the piece more decorative, a decal was transferred to the cover. A gilded ring surrounds the cover and the base of the box. Do not overlook a good Sandwich decorated piece because the transfer faces in the opposite direction. Decals were purchased by the sheet from outside sources and were changed from time to time. It in no way affects value. *Courtesy, Sandwich Glass Museum, Sandwich Historical Society*

3298 PRESSED OPAL OVAL BOX
1⅝" H. x 4" L. x 2½" W. 1873–1887

The meanings of words change over the years, so we must consider these changes in our study. The 1847 edition of Webster's dictionary describes *box* as "a case of any size and of any material". In 1872, *rectangular* was still not a prerequisite. American Flint Glass Workers Union records from Sandwich list several types of boxes: Quinlan, white boxes, new white boxes. Without catalogs, we cannot relate their listing to known sizes and shapes. The Boston and Sandwich Glass Company sloar book in 1887 listed Quinlan boxes as small as ¼ ounce. Many types of ointments and salves were marketed as well as patches used for "beauty spots" to hide facial scars of smallpox. Many containers found general secondary use after they were emptied. The base of this oval box is recessed ¼". Oval boxes also came with metal covers. *Courtesy, Sandwich Glass Museum, Sandwich Historical Society*

3299 PRESSED ROUGE BOXES
1¼" H. x 1¼" Dia. 1850–1887
These tiny pieces are sometimes sold as pill boxes or ring holders. We purchased one that had rouge in it. It would be difficult to transfer rouge from one container to another, so we believe this was the original use.

3300 PRESSED ROUGE BOX FRAGMENTS
(a) Blue green, chip on base
(b) Green, perfect
(c) Blue, destroyed rim
(d) Light blue cover
All of these pieces are dug fragments. The great assortment of colors is an indication of their popularity. They were made at very little cost because they were made from the puddles of good glass left toward the bottom of the batch after the bulk of the glass was used up. This was called "finishing out the pot". Some have a satin finish.

INVENTORY OF SANDWICH GLASS

No.	Description	Condition	Date Purchased	Amount	Date Sold	Amount

TOYS

1825–1897

The earliest glass houses in the United States devoted some part of their production to satisfying the needs of children. Glassworkers took home for their own children free-blown toys made during the idle time between batches. The toys were so loved that they soon became a regular part of a glassmaking day, and special child and doll-size molds were made so that toys could be commercially marketed. It was necessary for every glass house to include tiny items in their inventory. As each shop neared the bottom of a batch of glass, all of the glass was not usable. Pools of good glass remained that could be used for pieces such as eye cups or individual salts and toys. This was called "finishing out the batch".

On July 9, 1825, the first day that the Sandwich Glass Manufactory produced glass commercially, fifteen toy decanters were listed in the company record book. On July 30, 220 blown molded toy wines were produced at a cost of four cents each. Over one thousand toy articles were manufactured during July in the first three weeks of production. Included were tumblers and *jugs*, which was the term for pitchers. By August 1825, toy hats and toy patty-pans were added to the production line. A *patty* was a small pie—we would call it a tart. On June 23, 1827, Michael Doyle's shop made 166 blown molded, footed, toy lamps. Three styles of toy lamps were listed in July, and style number three was made with and without a handle. Heavy production of toys continued throughout the life of all four major companies—Sandwich Glass Manufactory, Boston and Sandwich Glass Company, Cape Cod Glass Works, and Cape Cod Glass Company—and the minor companies that attempted to reestablish the glass industry in the 1890's.

The first of the toys made at the Sandwich Glass Manufactory were free-blown and blown molded. Although we have fragments of this type of glass, it is virtually impossible to identify them as having been intended for a toy. However, by the second half of 1827, the pressing of glass became established, beginning with a thick cup-plate-like toy plate and advancing to a variety of doll-size tableware. Once pressing began at Sandwich, the manufacture of toys increased substantially, so that, today, large quantities of pressed toy items are available to the collector.

By 1830, a large percentage of adult glassware was being pressed in intricate patterns that had a stippled background. These ornate patterns, called *Lacy*, were duplicated in the pressing of toys. Floral motifs used on adult Lacy salts lent themselves to tiny dishes. Toy plates, vegetable dishes, bowls, and tureens were made in clear glass and several colors. A limited number of patterns predominated: diamonds, scrolls, leaves, lilies, roses, rosettes and fans. Several of these motifs were combined on one piece, such as diamonds and scrolls or diamonds, scrolls and lilies. Although the same pattern or combination of patterns might not appear on every piece, the various table pieces combined nicely to make a set of doll-size dishes that brought happiness to the little girl who was fortunate to own it.

During this period, the same shape used in Lacy toy dishes was also pressed in a pattern of simple panels. Variety was created by combining the panels with rayed bases or concentric rings. As the Lacy era came to an end in the 1850's, the style and character of toys kept pace with changes in the style of their adult-size counterparts. The patterns with stippled backgrounds were discontinued and replaced with a larger assortment of paneled pieces. Finally, even the patterned bases disappeared, giving way to plain ones. The simplest possible forms were used to mass produce large quantities of toys for the ever expanding American market.

As stated earlier, glass factories in Sandwich were not the only ones that devoted part of production to children's articles. The book *M'Kee Victorian Glass*, published by The Corning Museum of Glass, reproduces five catalogs of glassware manufactured by McKee and Brothers, a Pittsburgh company, between 1859 and 1871. Toy candlesticks and flat irons scaled for doll houses, identical to the Sandwich products, are illustrated, proving that identical molds were purchased from commercial mold makers and were filled with glass by different companies. This makes attribution of a random piece to a particular factory impossible unless its history can be traced and documented by family records, in lieu of glass company records. Experts who use catalogs as the only source of proof for origin are limiting their attribution to only one company, when other companies frequently made the same pieces.

Glass toys came in several sizes. Some were scaled for small dolls and doll houses, others for large dolls and play houses large enough for a child to enter and set up housekeeping. Still others were sized to a child's hands, such as lamps with working burners, and fair sized tumblers. The McKee catalogs show a fluted toy tumbler that holds ½ gill (four tablespoons or ¼ cup). This is twice the capacity of the tumbler we usually think of as a toy—the size often referred to as a "whiskey taster" that holds two tablespoons of liquid. Both of these tumblers are larger in scale than the Lacy cup and saucer. Yet all are listed as toys in the records, making it difficult for us to differentiate between pieces meant to be used by a child in play or at the dinner table and pieces intended as doll dishes.

In his book *The Romance of Old Sandwich Glass*, author Frank W. Chipman lists an inventory of molds belonging to the Boston and Sandwich Glass Company. The list was taken from original factory records. It is undated, but the mold for a General Grant cigar holder is included. Ulysses S. Grant was a General of the Union Army in the Civil War. He was elected President in 1868, so we conclude that the list is an inventory taken in the mid-1860's. The factory owned the following toy molds:

Centre bowl (Ed. note: a compote)
Pitcher
Decanter
Dish & cover
Nappie & top
Basin
Tureen
Sugar
Cream
Cup & saucer
Tumbler
Lemonade
Salt
Mustard

A Cape Cod Glass Company list of glass (reproduced in its entirety in Chapter 4) includes the following selection of toys. The list dates from 1864 to 1869, so it is not likely that any of the pieces would be Lacy.

Tumblers
Lemonades
Cups and Saucers
Sugars
Creams
Butters
Salts
Nappies, (3 in.)
Ewers and Basins
Decanters
Flat Irons
Oval Dishes
Candlesticks
Castor Bottles
Castors, (4 bottles)

The Cape Cod Glass Company was primarily a wholesale operation and sold most of its inventory in bulk. Toys were shipped by the box lot, not by the set. Catalogs from several glass companies indicate that, in the 1860's, the four-piece table set so important to collectors of adult tableware had not come into being. Sugars, creams, spoon holders, and butters (covered nappies) were sold individually and were not necessarily shown on the same page in the catalogs. The Cape Cod Glass Company did not list a toy spoon holder at all.

Note the listing of a 3" nappie. A *nappie* is a shallow bowl normally listed with full-size pressed pattern glass. The 3" nappie would be considered a scarce piece by a pattern glass collector and would not be considered at all by a toy collector. The Cape Cod list proves that the same piece had several uses. There are no illustrations, but this example raises another problem. Elsewhere in the Cape Cod document are listed 3" individual butters and 3" plates, in addition to 3" nappies. Were these pieces interchangeable with toys? Whatever the answer, it is clear that some pieces originally intended as toys have found their way into other categories and are now being admired as free-blown "courting lamps", blown molded "whiskey tasters", pressed cup plates, pressed Lacy salts, and pressed pattern honey dishes.

By the time the Boston and Sandwich Glass Company closed, the smallest scale toys were no longer in style. Toy four-piece table sets were marketed by Pittsburgh houses, but we find no evidence of Sandwich manufacture. Pressed toy tumblers are listed in a record book kept by members of the American Flint Glass Workers Union Local No. 16 that is dated 1879–1883. Manufacture of these tumblers and some larger scale toy caster bottles were continued by several glass companies that occupied the Boston and Sandwich Glass Company site, judging by the many poor-quality fragments that were found near the surface in the factory yard.

THESE SIMPLE HINTS WILL HELP YOU IDENTIFY SANDWICH TOYS.

Study the simple diamonds, lilies, roses, rosettes, leaves, scrolls and fans that are used on Lacy pieces and accept any combination of these patterns as a product of the Boston and Sandwich Glass Company.

Scallops on the rims and bases of Lacy pieces are all the same size.

If a tiny handle makes adult use awkward, the piece was intended to be a toy.

To identify use based on form, compare toys with their adult counterparts.

At antiques shows and flea markets, expect Sandwich toys to be mixed in with salts, shot glasses, penny candy scoops, cup plates, individual butter plates, nut dishes, and other similar small pieces—antique and contemporary.

On toy Sandwich candlesticks, the inside diameter of the socket is approximately ¼", much larger than the 3⁄16" diameter of a present-day birthday candle. If the hole in the socket is small, the piece was not made at Sandwich.

3301 FREE-BLOWN TOY HAND LAMP

1½" H. to top of neck 1825–1835

The dimensions of the font, the little handle and the size of the cork tube burner tell us that this lamp was meant for a child. Ignore the crimped trailing end of the applied handle and study just the portion that is held. The handle that would easily slip out of an adult hand would be comfortable between the thumb and fingers of a child. The tube is only ¹³⁄₁₆" long with an outside diameter of ³⁄₃₂". The tube has the tiniest slot for the needle-like pickwick used to raise the wick. Original factory documents prove that toy lamps were made in abundance and sold readily. Larger handled lamps for adults were called *chamber lamps*. We have no evidence in factory records of lamps specifically designed to be "courting" or "sparking" lamps. *The Bennington Museum, Bennington, Vermont*

3302 BLOWN MOLDED RIBBED TOY HAND LAMP *McKearin GI-7*

1⅛" H. to top of font; 2¼" Dia. 1825–1835

Early hand lamps made for children can be distinguished from small "courting" or night lamps by the size of the handle. If the hole will not take an adult finger, the lamp was made for a child. The amount of whale oil that this lamp would hold is limited. The glass was blown into a ribbed ball stopper mold, and reworked to form a melon font. The single tube burner is the earliest type used at Sandwich. It is held in place by the pressure of a cork stopper against the rim. According to writings of C. C. P. Waterman dated April 27, 1865, "Mr. Jarves invented the cork tubes for lamps which he sold to William Carleton (owner of a Boston lamp manufacturing business and a director of the Boston and Sandwich Glass Company) for $100." The tin plate through which the tube passes is marked "PATENT". *Courtesy, Sandwich Glass Museum, Sandwich Historical Society*

3303 BLOWN MOLDED TOY HAND LAMP

(a) Matching stopper 3⅜" H. x 2½" Dia.
(b) Toy hand lamp 2" H. 1828–1835

Toy lamps were often made from the same molds that were used to make decanter stoppers. The rayed pattern that is on the top of this stopper became the rayed base of the lamp. The glass that would have formed the plug of the stopper was sheared off, leaving a rim that was the right diameter for a tiny whale oil burner. The Bennington Museum also has a candlestick made from a stopper mold, which can be seen in photo 4001. *The Bennington Museum, Bennington, Vermont*

3304 BLOWN MOLDED DIAMOND DIAPER TOY LAMP

McKearin GII-18 2" H. x 1⅞" Dia. 1825–1826
This tiny lamp originated in a mold that had a band of diamond diapering around the center with bands of vertical ribs above and below. After the glass was removed from the mold, the piece was crimped below the diapered band to form the ribbed foot and drawn in at the top to form a rim to fit the tin whale oil burner. Subsequent photos show similar pieces that, when removed from the mold, were formed into a footed jug and a footed handled custard. Sixteen diamonds in a circle form the base pattern. Blown molded pieces that can be identified as toys from factory records command higher prices than their adult-size counterparts. *The Bennington Museum, Bennington, Vermont*

3305 FREE-BLOWN TOY LAMP WITH DIAMOND CHECK TOY PLATE BASE

4⅛" H. to top of font; 2⅜" Dia. 1828–1835
This is the child's version of the adult cup plate lamp. The base of this lamp was pressed in the 2⅛" Dia. Diamond Check toy plate mold. Note its thickness, indicating early manufacture. The solid knopped standard was free-blown as part of the font and applied to the center of the bottom of the plate. All early lamps with plate bases have a rough pontil mark underneath, on what would be the smooth upper surface of the plate. Cork tube whale oil burners are still often found on their lamps. *The Bennington Museum, Bennington, Vermont*

3306 FREE-BLOWN TOY LAMP WITH DIAMOND CHECK TOY PLATE BASE AND MALLORY LAMP GLASS

(a) Lamp 3⅞" H. x 2¼" Dia.
(b) Mallory lamp glass (chimney) 2½" H. x 1⅛" Dia. at bottom flare
(c) Combined size 6¼" H. x 2¼" Dia. 1828–1835
Here is the same lamp with the addition of an applied handle. The ridged collar, called a *cap* by the industry, was permanently fastened to the rim of the font. This was the earliest threaded collar used at Sandwich. A threaded whale oil burner was fitted to it, providing more stability than a cork tube burner. The blown cylindrical chimney was illustrated by Deming Jarves in a letter dated November 23, 1825. It was called a *Mallory lamp glass*. Today we would not allow a child to play with fire, but if children did not learn to handle open flame, they would be left with no light at all. They learned to respect fire at an early age, but reports of death due to accidents when handling lamps were common. *Courtesy, Sandwich Glass Museum, Sandwich Historical Society*

3307 BLOWN MOLDED RIBBED TOY TUMBLER

McKearin GI-6 1⅞" H. x 1¾" Dia. 1830–1835
The pattern of vertical ribs is the simplest of the blown molded geometric patterns. This makes attribution to the Boston and Sandwich Glass Company extremely difficult unless the piece is accompanied by documentation. The rim was reworked, wiping out the already shallow pattern. Often called a "whiskey taster" because of its present-day usage, it was listed as a toy tumbler in the company sloar book. *Courtesy, Sandwich Glass Museum, Sandwich Historical Society*

3308 BLOWN MOLDED DIAMOND DIAPER

McKearin GII-16
(a) Toy tumbler 1¾" H. x 1⅝" Dia.
(b) Toy hat salt 1¾" H. x 2" Dia. 1825–1830
Note that both pieces were blown in the same pattern. The bands of ribbing and diamond diapering are identical on the tumbler and the hat. The tumbler has a plain base with an open pontil mark, and the hat has concentric circles on the base. Both blown molded toy hats and hat salts are listed in company records. The Sandwich Glass Manufactory sloar book shows that 250 toy hats and 600 toy decanters were made from the same batch of glass. *Courtesy, Sandwich Glass Museum, Sandwich Historical Society*

3309 BLOWN MOLDED DIAMOND DIAPER TOY TAPER TUMBLER

McKearin GII-19 2½" H. x 1⅞" Dia. 1830–1835
If a piece was blown into a mold, the pattern can be felt on the inside of the piece because the hot glass conformed to the contours in the mold. This pattern was identified from fragments dug at the site of the Boston and Sandwich Glass Company. The bands of vertical ribbing and diamond diapering are similar to the tumbler shown previously, but a narrow band of diagonal ribbing was added. Blown molded pieces are generally named for the pattern in the widest band or the motif that is most dominant. Study this piece carefully—it has been reproduced.

3310 BLOWN MOLDED DIAMOND DIAPER TOY HANDLED CUSTARD

McKearin GII-19 1¾" H. x 1½" Dia. 1825–1826

There is no question that these small items were for children. The strap handle and the size of the bowl do not lend themselves to adult use. The bowl holds slightly over one tablespoon of liquid. The handle is attached to the bowl with such delicacy that it would be an easy matter to snap it off. Fragments in large quantities have been found matching the base and the rim in an area of the dump site at the factory that indicates very early production. If this piece had been made in 1900, it would be called a "punch cup". In earlier years, handled pieces shaped like egg cups were used for custard.

3311 BLOWN MOLDED SUNBURST TOY JUG

McKearin GIII-12 2¼" H. x 1¾" Dia. 1825–1826

This jug is about the same size as the handled custard. The base is similar to the fragments that accompany the custard. The wide band of pattern has two blocks of the sunburst motif and two blocks of diamond diapering. The rim was reworked to make a spout and the handle was applied. Note how much of the length of the handle was applied to the body. Reproductions of creamers made in the 1900's for *decorative* purposes have handles lightly attached to the body. *Courtesy of The Toledo Museum of Art (Acc. No. 71.23)*

3312 BLOWN MOLDED SUNBURST TOY JUG

McKearin GIII-12 2⅛" H. 1825–1835

It is difficult for us today to visualize these beautiful pieces in the hands of playful children. Keeping small children entertained until they were old enough to take on chores was a major part of a mother's day. Only the tiniest fingers could grasp this handle and make use of the jug's contents. This is a piece that was meant to be used—note how firmly the handle is attached. Blown molded toy jugs were listed in the company sloar book during the first month of glass production, July 1825. By the end of 1825, toys blown molded from blue glass were being made. *Courtesy, Sandwich Glass Museum, Sandwich Historical Society*

3313 BLOWN MOLDED SUNBURST TOY JUG

McKearin GIII-12 2⅛" H. 1825–1835

The earliest pieces were first crudely blown into a mold, then removed from the mold and finished by hand. How a piece was finished was left to the discretion of the worker. The blue Sunburst jug has a plain rim, but this clear jug has a rim folded to the inside. The blue piece shown above has a crimp above the curl at the bottom of the handle; this piece has only the curl. There are concentric circles on the base of the jug, but another otherwise identical jug may have a plain base. Minor differences in the patterned mold or in the hand finishing have little effect on value. However, with each passing year, the difference in value between clear and colored pieces becomes greater. *The Bennington Museum, Bennington, Vermont*

3314 BLOWN MOLDED DIAMOND SUNBURST TOY JUG

McKearin GIII-21 2¾" H. 1825–1835

Study the widest horizontal band of the pattern. It is divided into six panels. Three panels of tiny diamonds, called *diamond diapering*, alternate with three panels of a sunburst pattern. A diamond, divided into nine parts, is in the center of the sunburst. This diamond-centered sunburst indentifies the jug as *Diamond Sunburst*. It is always combined with bands of diagonal ribbing. This piece has a rayed base, but other pieces in the Diamond Sunburst pattern could have concentric circles on the base, a circle of diamonds, or no pattern at all. *The Bennington Museum, Bennington, Vermont*

3315 BLOWN MOLDED SUNBURST TOY DECANTER WITH HAND-FORMED SUNBURST STOPPER

McKearin GIII-12 3½" H. x 1⅝" Dia. 1825–1835

Deming Jarves' Sandwich Glass Manufactory opened its doors on July 4, 1825. The records show that toy decanters were made on the first full day of glassmaking, July 9. Note how the left side of the decanter is different from the right side. The mold slipped during production, causing the glass to seep into the seam and make a rounded rib the full length of the decanter. This gives the piece character and is not a defect. Articles that were blown into these early molds have soft mold marks, unlike the thin, sharp mold marks of pressed items. These early pieces have pontil marks.

3316 LACY TOY EWER AND BASIN
(a) Ewer 2½" H.
(b) Basin 1" H. x 3¼" Dia. 1835-1850
All of the pieces we call *Lacy* are pressed with a stippled background. Note the unique handle on the ewer with its three thorn-like protrusions. Note, too, the manner in which the forward part of the top of the handle is molded into the body. The mold mark can be seen on the side of the handle and across the thorn at the highest point of the handle. This is important, because it is a characteristic of the earliest pressed ewers. The body is circular, with a six-petaled rosette on each side. A basket of flowers is on each side of the lower part, and a band of flowers encircles the basin. When buying two-unit sets, make sure the color of each unit is an exact match. *Courtesy, Sandwich Glass Museum, Sandwich Historical Society*

3317 PRESSED PANELED TOY EWER AND BASIN
(a) Ewer 2½" H.
(b) Basin 1" H. x 3⅛" Dia. 1840-1855
The Lacy Period came to an end after an excellent grade of glass sand was discovered in Western Massachusetts. It was no longer necessary to hide defects with a stippled background. The intricate floral pattern was replaced by simple panels, although the shape of the ewer remained the same, even to the thorns on the handle.

3318 PRESSED PANELED TOY EWERS
(a) Amethyst
(b) Green 2⅜" H. 1845-1870
Where both handles reach their highest point there appears to be a chip. However, this is deliberate delineation in the mold seam just forward of the thorn. This mold seam, which, on the Lacy ewer, crossed the handle on the thorn, has been brought forward. This change in mold design caused the hot glass to seep into the juncture where all three mold pieces met, creating a roughness that looks like a chip. A mold mark continues down the outside of the handle to the base of the ewer. Another mold mark is directly opposite, from the center under the spout to the base. This tells us that the body was molded in two pieces. A third piece formed the upper surface of the spout and the forward part of the handle. The next step in the evolution of the ewer was to eliminate the thorns entirely. The Corning Museum of Glass has such a ewer in its collection. *Courtesy, Sandwich Glass Museum, Sandwich Historical Society*

3319 PRESSED PANELED TOY PITCHER AND BASIN

(a) Pitcher 2¼" H.
(b) Basin ⅞" H. x 3⅛" Dia. 1855–1870
Simplification continued as the ewer form was replaced by the pitcher, mirroring the style changes of adult porcelain and ironstone sets. The ornate handle was replaced by a simple one, and the spout was shortened. The panels begin at the base and continue to the rim without the interruption of the exaggerated horizontal convex band halfway down the ewer. This simple form increased productivity of the shops and kept the Sandwich glass industry competitive. *Courtesy, Sandwich Glass Museum, Sandwich Historical Society*

3320 LACY POINTED OVAL TOY TUMBLERS WITH CIRCULAR BASE

(a) Fiery opalescent
(b) Canary 1¾" H. x 1¾" Dia. 1830–1850
Toy tumblers in this pattern were quite popular. Many have survived and are still available in several colors. Pressed patterns with stippled backgrounds are called *Lacy* today. The base is smooth underneath and flares out to give the impression of a foot. The stippling begins above this flared base. Much thought was given to the making of this tumbler. The Pointed Oval pattern is repeated five times around the body, which was pressed in a three-part mold. All three mold marks can be seen in tumbler A. The pattern was repeated twice on two sections of the mold, while the third section of the mold repeated the pattern only once and was only half the width of the other sections. If you hold tumbler A up to the light, it resembles the red and yellow color that reflects from a fire opal gemstone.

3321 LACY POINTED OVAL TOY TUMBLERS

(a) Fiery opalescent, circular base 1¾" H. x 1¾" Dia.
(b) Blue-green, scalloped base 1¾" H. x 1⅝" Dia.
(c) Clear, circular base, bottom view 1¾" H. x 1¾" Dia. 1830–1850
Lacy Pointed Oval tumblers were also produced with a scallop on a slightly raised foot. This is the rarest of the child's tumblers. Despite years of searching, each scalloped foot tumbler we have seen has been found only in the beautiful blue-green shown in the center. The upper surface of the scallops are plain, but the concave base is rayed underneath to the outer edge of each scallop. The effect is that of a footed tumbler. All Sandwich lacy pieces were made by the Boston and Sandwich Glass Company. By the time the Cape Cod Glass Works was founded, lacy glass was out of favor.

3322 LACY HEART CHILDREN'S LEMONADE

2" H. x 2" Dia. 1830–1835

On May 28, 1830, Deming Jarves was issued a patent for an improvement in glassmakers' molds. "The improvement claimed is for the joining of a handle, or handles, or other similar projections, on glass cups, by pressure, at one operation, instead of attaching them to the cup after it has been blown, in the way heretofore practiced." This piece is the earliest known example of use of the 1830 patent. Only two Lacy Heart lemonades are recorded as being in existence at this time. Three hearts alternate with three fleur-de-lys variants. This production method was used to make the Lacy Peacock Eye mustard, an item not as rare as this Heart piece. *The Bennington Museum, Bennington, Vermont*

3323 PRESSED PANELED TOY TUMBLERS

1⅝" H. x 1⅝" Dia. 1845–1870

Because the use of a piece can change over the years, we may assign it to the wrong category. Today, for example, most toy tumblers would be called "whiskey tasters" by collectors because they are the size of the small shot glasses we use now to measure liquor. Many items originally listed as toys have taken on different identification. The 3" nappie that was a part of adult tableware was also included in toy listings but are not seen in glass toy collections now. When you are at a flea market or antiques show, look for toy tumblers mixed in with contemporary shot glasses, especially in clear glass.

3324 PRESSED PANELED TOY TUMBLER FRAGMENTS

(a) Whole tumbler fragment
(b) Assembled from three fragments 1⅝" H. x 1⅝" Dia. 1845–1870

Both tumblers were dug at the Boston and Sandwich Glass Company site. Tumbler A had been discarded because it had an underfill at the base. Tumbler B had an underfill on the rim. Sufficient fragments were found to prove without a doubt that they were made in Sandwich. Underfill resulting from not enough glass pressed into the mold does not detract from value today. We think of underfill and overfill as something that gives our glass character.

3325 PRESSED PRISM PANEL

(a) Blue opalescent toy tumbler
(b) Amethyst toy lemonade 1¾" H. x 1¾" Dia.
1859–1869

Fragments of these pieces in these colors were found at the Cape Cod Glass Company site. Unfortunately, that Company's list of glassware does not identify toys by pattern name, but a King Glass Company catalog shows tumbler A as *Prism*. We are adding the word *Panel* to differentiate it from Prism pattern adult tableware, which is not paneled. In the East, small tumblers with handles were known as *lemonades*. They were not mugs. Mugs were handled pieces that are smaller in diameter at the top than at the base. The pattern and color of tumbler A (not the size) was used to make the hat cover for the Cavalier pomade shown in Chapter 9. *Courtesy, Sandwich Glass Museum, Sandwich Historical Society*

3326 PRESSED FLUTE TOY LEMONADE

1⅝" H. x 1⅝" Dia. 1840–1870

This lemonade is divided into nine flutes that come only half way up the side. The handle was pressed in one piece with the body and is in the middle of a flute. Note the excess glass inside the handle, called overfill. It may appear at any point along a seam where the mold is worn. Overfill does not change the value. *Courtesy, Sandwich Glass Museum, Sandwich Historical Society*

3327 PRESSED FLUTE TOY LEMONADE

1⅝" H. x 1⅝" Dia. 1840–1870

Here is the nine-flute lemonade accompanied by fragments dug at the Boston and Sandwich Glass Company. This is the only configuration of pressed lemonade handle that we can document as Sandwich. Clear glass lemonades are sometimes sold as penny candy scoops, and find their way into collections of store and advertising items.

3328 PRESSED FINE RIB (REEDED)
(a) Toy tumbler
(b) Toy lemonade 1¾" H. x 1¾" Dia. 1850–1870

The pattern we call Fine Rib was listed as Reeded by the companies that made it. A New England Glass Company catalog illustrates many patterns, including Reeded, that were also made at Sandwich. The smallest tumblers and lemonades shown in full-size tableware hold ⅓ pint (⅔ cup). The smallest in the Cape Cod Glass Company list is ½ gill (¼ cup). These pieces hold half that. "Whiskey tasters" are not listed, nor are they listed in the Pittsburgh area catalogs we have studied. Note how the ribs come almost to the rim, matching the rim of the fragment dug at the Boston and Sandwich Glass Company. The handle on the lemonade was applied after the piece was removed from a toy tumbler mold. Note the size of the opening, which only a child's hand could use.

3329 PRESSED FINE RIB WITH BAND TOY TUMBLERS
(a) Transparent blue-green
(b) Translucent blue 1¾" H. x 1⅝" Dia. 1850–1870

This pattern is the same shown previously with a ³⁄₁₆" band surrounding the rim. The fragment is one of many dug at the Boston and Sandwich Glass Company site that matches the band and reeding of the whole tumbler. This tumbler is more likely to be found in a variety of colors than in clear, unlike the plain Fine Rib without the band. Toy pieces in color are considerably more valuable than clear.

3330 BLOWN CHILDREN'S MUG ENGRAVED "WARREN"
3" H. x 2¼" Dia. January 14, 1863

Henry F. Spurr, general manager of the Boston and Sandwich Glass Company in the 1880's, had a son Warren, who was born January 14, 1861. Warren was given this piece on his second birthday. The design engraved around the rim, the wreath and the eight-pointed stars can be seen on a Late Blown goblet in photo 4245 in Volume 4. Without the engraving, this piece would have been sold as an adult lemonade.

3331 BLOWN CHILDREN'S MUG ENGRAVED "BABY"

3" H. x 2½" Dia. 1860–1870

Descendants of the Lapham family have many pieces made at the Boston and Sandwich Glass Company for the Lapham children. Sometimes the children watched the engraver, who then presented the piece to the child as a memento of his visit. Sandwich engravers used six-pointed and eight-pointed stars to fill in the background after the border design, lettering, and wreath had been completed. The stars were quickly made by striking the side of the piece either three or four times. These copper wheel engraved designs were used until the company closed, but later pieces were blown much thinner than the one shown here.

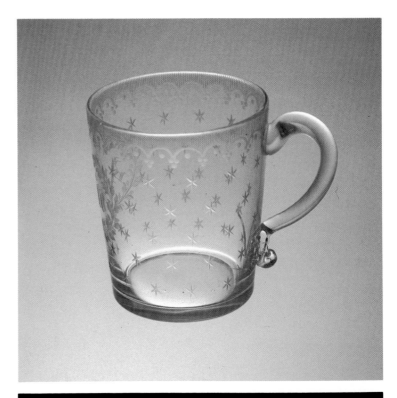

3332 LATE BLOWN CHILDREN'S MUG ENGRAVED "BABY"

2⅛" H. x 2⅛" Dia. February 17, 1883

According to Sandwich Glass Museum records, this piece was made by Nathaniel Ham(b)len. The lettering and date are surrounded by a copper wheel engraved wreath of rosettes and ferns. It is interesting to study the use of various sizes of drinking vessels during different time periods. If this piece were not engraved, most experts would identify it as a "handled whiskey taster". But a study of the Boston and Sandwich Glass Company 1874 catalog shows a similar piece listed as a *children's mug*. Rays cut into the base were called *star bottom* in the catalog. *Courtesy, Sandwich Glass Museum, Sandwich Historical Society*

3333 FREE-BLOWN TOY PATTY-PAN

1⅜" H. x 3" Dia. 1825–1835

Whether glass or tin, a pan has sloping sides and a flat bottom. They ranged in size from large adult utility milk pans to this toy version that was in production by August 1825. The rim is folded to the outside, away from the surface that would be in contact with food. *Patties* were small pies, called tarts today. Were the toy pans for real food or mud pies? *The Bennington Museum, Bennington, Vermont*

3334 PRESSED HEXAGONAL TOY SPOON HOLDERS

(a) Translucent green

(b) Clear 1¾" H. x 1½" Dia. 1850–1870

These spoon holders have found their way into collections of "whiskey tasters" and even salts. When recognized as children's pieces, however, they are usually identified as tumblers, even though the proportions more closely resemble an adult spoon holder. Many toy spoon holders have survived. The clear one is the most common of all toy pieces. Keep in mind they have more value as toy pieces than as adult pieces. When searching for this piece, look for the two rows of horizontal ribbing and the round base.

3335 PRESSED HEXAGONAL TOY SPOON HOLDER

1¾" H. x 1¼" Dia. 1850–1870

This spoon holder has six panels that extend onto the foot. Note the roughness of the inside edge of the rim, indicating rapid release from the mold. Toys were produced in great quantity, and were not fire polished or reworked in any way. Rough mold seams are not chips and do not reduce value.

3336 LACY TOY JUGS

(a) Opaque blue, scalloped base 1¾" H.

(b) Clear, circular base 1⅝" H. 1835–1850

Pitchers were called *jugs* in the early 1800's. Toy jugs were used by children to serve milk. Jug B is the most common of the Lacy pattern toys and is easily recognized by the shape of the spout and the unusually large flanged rim. The handle was molded with the body. A mold mark runs up the outside of the handle and another divides the spout. To minimize the seam under the spout, corrugations were put along the edge of each mold piece, resulting in a zipper-like effect. A third piece of the mold formed the top of the spout and the flanged rim. The pattern combines a diamond and scroll motif with a lily. A variation of jug A has a smaller spout with a scalloped rim. *Courtesy, Sandwich Glass Museum, Sandwich Historical Society*

3337 LACY TOY CUP AND SAUCER

(a) Cup 1" H. x 1⅛" Dia.
(b) Saucer ⅜" H. x 1⅞" Dia. 1835–1850
This cup matches the toy jug shown previously and was molded in the same manner, even to the "zipper" that minimizes the mold mark. The diamond and scroll with lily pattern is on each side of the cup. This cup was also made with a solid, small, five-lobed handle. The saucer that always accompanies the cup does not match in pattern. Diamonds and roses are in the center, surrounded by a band of roses and rosettes. The same shape of cup and saucer was also made in a plain paneled pattern.

3338 LACY TOY BOWL ON LOW FOOT

1" H. x 1⅝" Dia. 1835–1850
The bowl in the photo is fiery opalescent, but it can be found in clear and a variety of colors. As with most glass toys, it is difficult to find this piece without damage because it had hard use as a plaything. The pattern of diamond and scroll with lily is repeated three times around the bowl, on each of three mold pieces. There is no pattern on the foot.

3339 LACY TOY OVAL BOWL

¾" H. x 1⅞" L. x 1¼" W. 1835–1850
The lily motif is well known on adult Sandwich Lacy pieces and is repeated on many toy pieces, combined with a diamond and scroll. There is a single row of beading around the scalloped rim and no design on the base. Lacy toys tend to be thicker than the later paneled pieces, and while minor flakes are acceptable, major chipping takes away value. Keep in mind that toys are often mistaken for adult salts and nut dishes, so they have been assimilated into those categories. This bowl in particular is included in salt collections. When large salt collections come up for sale, check them for children's glass. *Courtesy, Sandwich Glass Museum, Sandwich Historical Society*

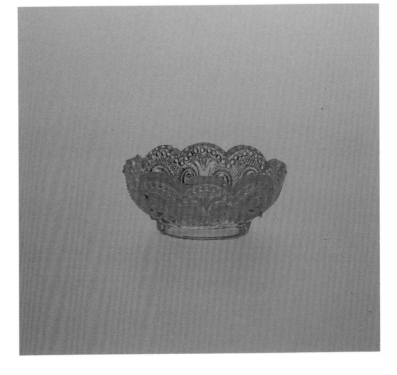

3340 LACY TOY OVAL DISH

½" H. x 3" L. x 2" W. 1835–1850

The ½" height of this dish did not allow the use of the lily, so it was eliminated from the diamond and scroll pattern. Tiny rose leaves were placed between the scrolls, and rosettes inside the curl of the scrolls. This piece is fiery opalescent and dates from the late 1830's. The coloring resembles an opal gemstone and was accomplished by using a special formula that reacted to the reheating of clear glass after it was taken out of the mold. Do not look for mold marks running up the sides through the stippling. Shallow pieces were made by using a one piece mold and a plunger. Scallops on the rims of Sandwich toys are all the same size.

3341 LACY TOY OVAL DISHES

(a) Amethyst ½" H. x 3" L. x 2" W.
(b) Amber ⅝" H. x 3" L. x 2" W. 1835–1850

These oval dishes are the same as the fiery opalescent dish shown previously. Note the diamond and scroll pattern on the base. A row of beading is around the base. Rose leaves can be seen between the scrolls above the base. Chips as large as the ones on dish B seriously hurt the value. Some of the toy dishes are too large in scale to be used in doll houses, but they were the correct size for the larger play houses. Play houses were high enough for small children to stand up in. None of these dishes were "miniatures". They were produced for children's use, not display. *Courtesy, Sandwich Glass Museum, Sandwich Historical Society*

3342 PRESSED TOY PLATE

⅝" H. x 2¾" Dia. 1827–1835

The first of the pressed toy plates were thick and very crude. There are two such pressed patterns that can be attributed to the Boston and Sandwich Glass Company without question—this piece and the Diamond Check toy plate that was sometimes used as a foot for a toy lamp. The base is rayed. There is a pattern of concentric rings on the underside of the rim. A pattern of prisms is pressed into the upper surface of the rim. The lines of the prisms crossing the concentric rings give a diamond effect. Because a pattern was pressed into the upper surface all the way to the outer edge, they were easily damaged. Note the diameter of the plate. If you find a larger version, it is a cup plate. Later toy plates and cup plates were smooth on the upper surface. *Courtesy, Sandwich Glass Museum, Sandwich Historical Society*

3343 PRESSED DIAMOND CHECK TOY PLATE
¼" H. x 2⅛" Dia. 1828–1835

This toy plate is often used as a base for a toy lamp. The lamp is not too difficult to find, but the plate alone is rare. When this plate was used for a lamp base, it was turned upside down, and, while hot, the stem of the lamp was applied into the Diamond Check pattern on the bottom of the plate. Look at the plate in the photo. The upper surface is smooth and the pattern shows through. There are two concentric rows of pattern on the rim. *The Bennington Museum, Bennington, Vermont*

3344 LACY TOY PLATES
(a) Canary, concentric rings
(b) Clear, band of rosettes ¼" H. x 2¼" Dia.
    1835–1850

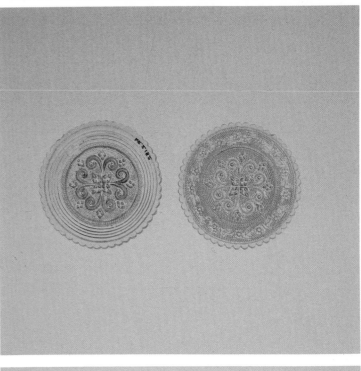

Although plate A is slightly more than 2" across, it carries all the features of adult pieces—concentric rings, Lacy pattern with stippling, and a ridged bottom. The ridge, which is the part that rests on the table, has tiny diagonal cuts that make a cable (rope) pattern. Note that the scallops on the rim are not damaged. This is unusual because they were commonly chipped when the plate was removed from the mold. Slight chipping that does not penetrate beyond the scallops should not deter from the value. Plate B has the same diamond and scroll center, surrounded by a sophisticated band of leaves and rosettes. *Courtesy, Sandwich Glass Museum, Sandwich Historical Society*

3345 LACY TOY NAPPIES ON HIGH FOOT
(a) Correct base with mold properly filled
(b) Small base from underfilled mold 2" H. x 1⅞"
    Dia. 1835–1850

A *nappie* was a shallow bowl with a flat base. If a nappie was put on a high or a low standard, the result was a piece we would call a "compote" today. Lacy pieces are pressed and usually quite thick, which allows them to withstand much abuse. The footed nappie on the left has the proper base. The small base of the nappie on the right was caused by underfilling the mold. Not enough glass was used at the time of pressing. Underfill does not change the value of a piece. Note the knop in the center of the standard. *Courtesy, Sandwich Glass Museum, Sandwich Historical Society*

3346 LACY TOY VEGETABLE DISHES ON FOOT
(a) Large, scalloped rim, ribbed foot
    1⅜" H. x 2¾" L. x 1⅞" W.
(b) Small, plain rim, scalloped foot
    1" H. x 1⅞" L. x 1¼" W. 1835–1850

The pattern on dish A consists of several elements. Scrolls surrounded the sidewalls below the scalloped rim, interrupted on each of the four sides by a three-leaved motif that resembles a fleur-de-lys. A beaded swag loops from corner to corner on the two long sides. A tiny lily and diamond covers the narrow panels making up the four corners. This piece is in scale with the largest of the Lacy toy dishes, but may have seen double duty as an adult salt. The scallops on the rim are the same width as the scallops on the base of dish B. The dimensions of the base of dish A approximate the rim of dish B. There is no doubt that both were the product of the same mold maker. Lilies cover the corner and end panels of dish B. All of the pieces we have studied are rough on the plain rim where the mold was opened. It, too, may have had another function as a toy salt.

3347 LACY TOY TUREEN
(a) Tureen 1¼" H. x 3" L. x 1⅞" W.
(b) Cover ¾" H. x 2¾" L. x 2" W.
(c) Combined size 2" H. x 3" L. x 2" W. 1835–1850

At first glance, Sandwich Lacy toy pieces seem to have varied patterns that do not match each other. It is true that there are several motifs, but they are combined so that each motif becomes an element in an overall pattern. The tureen is the only Lacy piece with a fan, but to the fan are added all the other elements. Each side of the fan extends into a scroll. A lily is at the end of each scroll and a rosette is centered in the curl of each scroll. There are two rosettes on the base. Their six petals are the same as that on the ewer in photo 3316. Here they are surrounded by a cable. Fans and scrolls are on the cover, and a row of beading surrounds a quatrefoil finial. This tureen should have a tray that matches in color. There is also a larger size toy tureen. *Courtesy, Sandwich Glass Museum, Sandwich Historical Society*

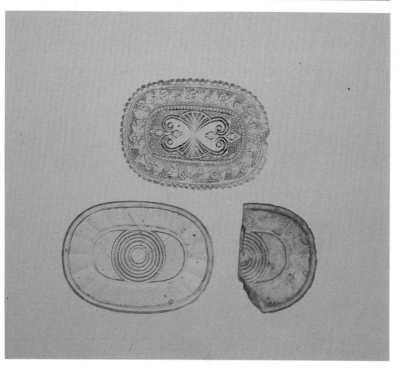

3348 PRESSED TOY TRAYS FOR TUREENS
(a) Lacy ⅜" H. x 2¾" L. x 1⅞" W.
(b) Paneled ⅜" H. x 2¾" L. x 2" W. 1835–1850

Tray A was made to be used with the Lacy tureen. Fans and scrolls are in the center, and diamonds have been added. The ridge that rests on the table has a cable pattern. There is a band of leaves with large and small rosettes — no roses. Even scallops make up the edge. We believe tray B was meant to be combined with a pressed paneled tureen. We have never located one, but it could very well be in a salt collection without its cover and tray. For a tureen, the distinguishing feature is two curled handles. We have seen the paneled tray combined with the Lacy tureen, but if you find such a mixture, you can be sure the pieces were combined at a later date. A married set does not have the value of a set that was assembled at the time of its manufacture. The fragment was dug at the Boston and Sandwich Glass Company site and is one of many found.

3349 PRESSED PANELED

(a) Toy plate, concentric circles ¼" H. x 2¼" Dia.
1835–1850
(b) Toy nappie, rayed base ½" H. x 2" Dia.
1850–1870

Plate A is flat with eighteen panels and concentric circles on the base. The two marks on the left are airtrapped bubbles. They do not deter from the value of the plate unless the bubble breaks out. B is a nappie, or shallow bowl. Note its rayed center. It is not a star—the rays extend to the edge of the bottom. The nappie has fourteen panels. The panels on both pieces are approximately the same width. In larger sizes, the center dimension was changed and the number of panels increased. The tureen tray has twenty panels.

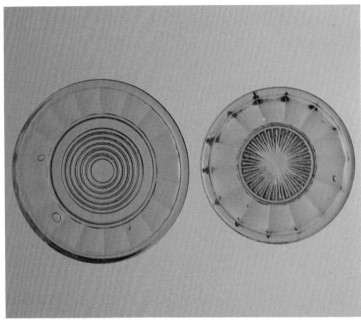

3350 PRESSED TOY BOWLS

(a) Large paneled, on foot 1⅜" H. x 2" Dia.
(b) Small fluted ¾" H. x 1¼" Dia. 1850–1870

The simple lines of the paneled and fluted pieces were used throughout this period. The Lacy Period had come to an end, and the pressed floral and geometric patterns that were fashionable during the last quarter of the century were not made in Sandwich. Note the lack of pattern on the foot of bowl A, which has fourteen panels. The base of B is also plain. This twelve-flute piece is usually combined with the paneled nappie in photo 3349 to make a handleless cup and deep saucer. Even though paneled dishes were produced after Lacy ones, there are less of them now. Look for bowl A in salt collections. *Courtesy, Sandwich Glass Museum, Sandwich Historical Society*

3351 PRESSED PANELED TOY SUGAR BOWL

(a) Bowl 1⅛" H. x 1⅜" Dia.
(b) Cover 1" H. x 1½" Dia.
(c) Combined size 2" H. x 1½" Dia. 1850–1870

Panels are simply and quickly pressed, yet give a piece some design quality. Twelve panels are on the bowl and there is no pattern on the foot. The cover has twelve matching panels that stop short of the circular nippled finial. Although these details are obvious in the photo, either unit separately could easily be overlooked in an antiques shop. Paneled pieces are often thought to be of twentieth century manufacture. The bowl alone might be considered a Midwest salt or nut dish. The cover might find its way into a box of odd parts or stoppers. The rule for quality stoppers holds true for toy covers—do not be afraid to purchase the cover alone. The bottom unit will eventually surface, and most of the value of the complete piece is in the cover. *Courtesy, Sandwich Glass Museum, Sandwich Historical Society*

3352 PRESSED PANELED TOY NAPPIE

(a) Nappie bottom unit ⅞" H. x 1¾" Dia.
(b) Cover 1⅛" H. x 1¾" Dia.
(c) Combined size 1¾" H. x 1¾" Dia. 1850–1870

The raised base gives the impression of a deep bowl, but this piece may have been the paneled version of a shallow nappie. With a cover, it may have been used for butter, but we are speculating. There are eleven panels on the nappie and cover. The panels on the cover are stepped down from the smooth center, which has a plain finial. A band around the cover matches the band on the nappie. *Courtesy, Sandwich Glass Museum, Sandwich Historical Society*

3353 PRESSED PRISM PANEL

(a) Sugar bowl without cover 1⅜" H. x 1⅜" Dia.
(b) Salt 1" H. x 1" Dia. 1860–1875

These two pieces are interesting to study. There is no doubt that they are toys. The larger piece has the form of a sugar bowl. If that was its intent, then the small piece must be a salt. Salts were listed in the Cape Cod Glass Company inventory, but we do not know of any actual salt identified as such by any authority on children's glass. This "salt" was dug from the Boston and Sandwich Glass Company site. It has a high lead content and was made in the same manner as a flat iron and candlestick. The bottom was ground flat to take away excess glass by which it was attached to a center fountain. The larger piece was pressed by a more sophisticated method and is concave under the foot.

3354 PRESSED PRISM PANEL TOY BUTTER

(a) Nappie bottom unit ½" H. x 2⅛" Dia.
(b) Cover ⅞" H. x 1¾" Dia.
(c) Combined size 1½" H. x 2⅛" Dia. 1860–1875

These pieces were made later than the paneled pieces that follow the lines of Lacy toys. Like the paneled dishes without prisms, the panels remain the same width on a larger piece, but the number of panels increases. There are ten plain panels alternating with ten prism panels on the bottom unit and the cover, yet it is obvious that the butter matches the footed pieces that have six plain panels alternating with six prism panels. It would be easy to miss the nappie bottom unit if it were on a sale table with inexpensive, pressed, adult, individual salts. *Courtesy, Sandwich Glass Museum, Sandwich Historical Society*

3355 BLOWN MOLDED PANELED TOY CASTER BOTTLES

(a) Pepper (perforated metal shaker cap)
 3" H. x 1" Dia.
(b) Mustard (pressed cover) 3" H. x 1" Dia.
(c) Bitter (metal tube with screw cap)
 3⅜" H. x 1" Dia.
(d) Cruet (pressed stopper) 3¾" H. x 1" Dia.
 1870–1887

These bottles were blown into a three-piece mold. Each bottle has nine panels, with three panels between each mold mark. The metal bitter bottle top is marked "LARKIN CO. BUFFALO N. Y." The Larkin Company manufactured soap and promoted its sale through the use of premiums such as this caster set. Many other glass factories in the East and Midwest produced identical toy caster bottles during this period, but the bottles dug at the Sandwich site that were damaged during manufacture prove their Sandwich origin.

3356 BLOWN MOLDED TOY CASTER BOTTLES

(a) Pepper (perforated metal shaker cap)
 3⅛" H. x 1" Dia.
(b) Mustard (pressed cover) 3" H. x 1" Dia.
(c) Cruet (pressed stopper) 3¾" H. x 1" Dia.
 1870–1897

Here is "SHERWOOD'S SQUARE TOY Caster" set exactly as pictured on the label of its original box. The mustard has a pressed glass cover, but the set is sometimes found with a metal cover with a finial. The pepper and mustard on the right were two of many bottles dug at the site of the Boston and Sandwich Glass Company. A variation of the stoppered cruet was dug that has a wide lip pulled down on opposite sides. The pressed cruet stopper in the foreground was also dug at the site. Because these caster bottles and the following ones are large in scale, and some were made from glass with no lead content, we are assigning them to the Boston and Sandwich Glass Company and one of the several glass companies that occupied the site after the Boston and Sandwich Glass Company closed.

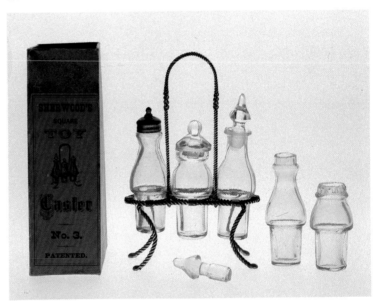

3357 BLOWN MOLDED TOY CASTER BOTTLES

(a) Pepper (perforated metal shaker cap)
 3⅜" H. x 1" Dia.
(b) Mustard (pressed cover) 3⅛" H. x 1" Dia.
(c) Cruets (pressed stoppers) 3¾" H. x 1" Dia.
 1870–1897

Doris Anderson Lechler in her book *Children's Glass Dishes, China, and Furniture* shows the box to this set. It is labeled "SHERWOOD'S PATENT TOY Caster. Four Bottles". To determine the use of toy pieces, remember that they are the same as their counterparts in adult tableware. *Peppers*, *mustards*, and *cruets* are the terms used on a Cape Cod Glass Company list under "Common Castor Bottles". A Pittsburgh glass company lists *vinegars* rather than *cruets*. Salt shakers were not part of a caster set. Most glass companies sold toy caster bottles, both in sets with the stand and in bulk to manufacturers like Sherwood, who would put them in their stands and box them for retail sale.

3358 BLOWN MOLDED RIBBON BAND TOY CASTER BOTTLES
(a) Pepper 3¾" H. x 1¼" Dia.
(b) Mustard 3½" H. before finishing 3¼" H. x 1¼" Dia. final size
(c) Cruet 3¾" H. x 1¼" Dia. 1880–1897

These caster bottles are never thought of as having been made in Sandwich. If only the three pieces shown here in this pattern had been dug at the factory site, we would concur, but many more were found. Bottle B is exactly as it came out of the mold. It was discarded before it was completed. Note the ridge around the neck ¼" down from the rim. The top of the bottle should have been sheared off at this point to accept a metal or pressed glass mustard cover. Bottle A has been sheared and should have a perforated metal shaker cap. Bottle C should have a pressed stopper.

3359 PRESSED TOY MUSTARD COVERS
(a) Paneled
(b) Round with paneled finial ⅞" H. x ⅞" Dia. 1870–1897

Many covers that were made to fit the toy mustard bottles from the caster sets were dug at the site of the Boston and Sandwich Glass Company. Cover A was probably dropped while it was being machined. It must have been very difficult to hold. A slight gouging by the cutter's wheel can be seen on the plug. Cover B still has a large part of the wheel mold fountain still attached, which proves that it had to have been made at the Boston and Sandwich Glass Company site.

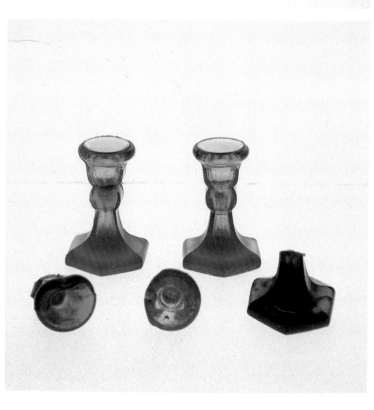

3360 PRESSED TOY CANDLESTICKS
1½" H. x 1" Dia. 1850–1870

Candlesticks for dollhouse tables were very popular. To date, this is the only one that can be documented, from fragments, as having been made unquestionably at Sandwich, although it was also made by McKee and Brothers in Pittsburgh. Six panels begin at the hexagonal base and end with six flutes on the socket, which has a round rim. If the candlestick is an old one, the hole in the socket will be the depth and diameter of an eraser on a common pencil. If the socket is small enough to hold a modern birthday candle, the candlestick was not made in Sandwich. The Cape Cod Glass Company included toy candlesticks in a list of glassware, and the fragments shown here were dug at the site of the Boston and Sandwich Glass Company. Candlesticks were pressed in a wheel mold. The bases were attached to a center "hub" from which the hot metal was forced into each candlestick mold. In the pair shown here, not enough glass went into each mold. The holes in the sockets extend down through the knops and into the bases.

3361 PRESSED TOY FLAT IRONS

(a) Blue-violet, side view
(b) Green, bottom view ⅞" H. x 1⅜" L. 1850–1870

This iron was the only toy utensil produced commercially at Sandwich that was not meant to be placed on a table. Irons were made in a mold in a manner similar to the pressing of stoppers on a stopper wheel. They were attached to the fountain (hub) of the wheel at their back end. When they were broken away from the fountain, a rough extension of glass was left on the back of the iron. This excess glass was machined away and polished. Sometimes the mold mark that runs through the center of the bottom was polished, but not much time was spent on this procedure. The Boston and Sandwich Glass Company and the Cape Cod Glass Company both made flat irons. Irons were also manufactured by McKee and Brothers in Pittsburgh, Pennsylvania, where they were called *toy sad irons*.

3362 SOUVENIR BRACELETS

(a) Blue and white 2¼" Dia.
(b) Red, green, white and goldstone 2½" Dia.
(c) Red, green, blue, white and goldstone 2½" Dia.
   1876

When Sandwich celebrated the Fourth of July, its glass companies entered a float in the parade. On the float was a replica of a glass furnace. Wood was aboard to stoke a fire, and gaffers and their helpers simulated the making of glass. Boxes of ready-made trinkets were hidden on the wagon and warmed up, then passed out to children. Bracelets made from imported glass rods were given to little girls. The three shown here were recovered from the 1876 Centennial parade. They were picked from the ground together with some souvenir roosters.

3363 FREE-FORMED SOUVENIR HEN

2½" H. 1876

A parade in a glassmaking town must have been a beautiful sight. Glassworkers hung glass ornaments from their clothing and sprinkled themselves with ground glass particles. Colorful glass balls were inserted into the muzzles of the rifles carried by the militia who accompanied the parade. Smoke pouring out of the simulated furnace chimney made many a boy believe that his souvenir hen had been made before his very eyes. A boxful of souvenirs picked up after the 1876 Centennial parade in Sandwich and hidden away for one hundred years revealed these delightful bird and bracelet trinkets.

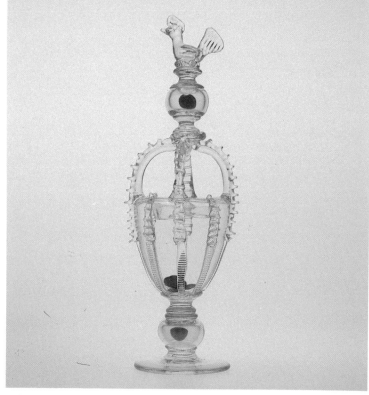

3364 FREE-FORMED BIRD WHIMSEY

6½" H. x 3⅛" Dia. 1840–1887

Odd pieces that were not made for commercial purposes are called *whimsies* because they are thought to have been made by a gaffer in his spare time. Many of them were, but many others were made to be given to children at holiday parades. Some were simple bird-forms with only the semblance of a head and tail. Others were sophisticated ornaments made up of a swan or rooster on a three to seven-knopped standard which could be used for a paperweight. This piece belongs to the family of James Lloyd and Hiram Dillaway. Similar birds were used as finials on glass banks.

3365 MONEY BOX WITH ROOSTER FINIAL

11¼" H. x 3" Dia. 1845

Banks were called *money boxes* in factory records. They are very rare today because their coins cannot be removed without breaking the glass. The bank has the form of a hollow-knopped goblet. A glass plate with a slot covers the bowl section. It is easy to drop coins into the slot, but an inside flange makes it impossible to slide them back out. The bank was assembled from five units. The base was made, then a hollow knop was blown, enclosing an 1844 half dime that moves freely inside the knop. The money box unit consists of the bowl with its slotted plate and the rods with rigaree arched over the top. Two units make up the finial, another hollow knop encloses an 1845 half dime, all surmounted with a free-form rooster. The units are held to each other with wafers. Inside the bank are ten 1853 three-cent pieces and one 1863 Indian head penny. This particular piece can be traced back to the family of James Lloyd.

3366 CUT TOY BOOKS

(a) Green canary from the family of Hiram Dillaway
    1⅛" H. x ⅞" W. 1840–1860
(b) Vasa Murrhina from the family of Charles W.
    Spurr 1" H. x ½" W. 1883–1884
(c) Dark ruby fragment dug at the Boston and
    Sandwich Glass company site. ¾" H. x ½" W.
    1850–1860

Unlike the larger cut book paperweights, little books were not a commercial product. Glass cutters used pieces of broken annealed glass, cut them into rectangular blanks, and then made the cuts that would turn them into little books. Some were presented to their loved ones as a token of affection. Others were given to their children to use as playthings. Books fashioned from beautiful glass are likely to have simple cuttings. All three have straight cuts on the covers and spine, and serrated edges called *beading*. Book B is exquisite. It has three layers of glass: Vasa Murrhina front cover, clear pages, and a blue back cover. Three edges of the book are concave to represent the pages.

3367 VASA MURRHINA CUT TOY BOOK FRAGMENT
1¼" H. x 1" W. 1883–1884

This book was dug at the site of Nehemiah Packwood's cutting shop on Willow Street, across the street from the site of the Vasa Murrhina Art Glass Company. The cutting shop was in operation from 1900 to 1922. At that time it was possible to pick up large fragments of beautiful glass simply by walking around any of the factory sites, so the date of the cutting may not coincide with the date of production of the glass. This holds true for all of the little books. The study of the Vasa Murrhina Art Glass Company and the Packwood cutting shops are in Volume 4 of this series.

3368 CUT OVERLAY TOY BOOK
1¼" H. x ⅞" W. 1874–1887

This book is from the John B. Vodon family collection and is believed to have belonged to one of his children. Vodon was an engraver who came to work for the Boston and Sandwich Glass Company in the early 1870's. The red overlay glass is good quality, but the cutting isn't. Vodon's three sons all became glass cutters, so it is possible that this piece was a first attempt by one of them. If so, the cutting could date from after the closing of the Boston and Sandwich Glass Company. Understand that, if you were to find this piece at an antiques show or flea market, there would be no way to attribute it to a particular glass factory. Only documented family pieces from family collections can be attributed with certainty. Vodon went on to establish his own cutting and engraving shop at Spring Hill in Sandwich. For information on glass cut and engraved by J. B. Vodon and Son, see Volume 4.

3369 CUT TOY BOOK FRAGMENT
2" H. x 1½" W. 1900–1922

It is thought that simple books with scant detail were meant to be used as the "family Bible" in a little girl's doll house. Fragments cut into book shapes were dug in areas known to have been used as a dump by the Boston and Sandwich Glass Company in the 1830's, showing that books for toys and larger book paperweights were made over the entire period that glass was cut in Sandwich. This book fragment was excavated from the Willow Street site of Nehemiah Packwood's cutting shop.

3370 CUT TOY BOOKS
(a) Octagon Diamond 1½" H. x 1¼" W. 1870–1887
(b) Checkered Diamond fragment 1" H. x ¾" W. 1870–1887
(c) Alternate Block Diamond 1" H. x ¾" W. 1888–1891
(d) Nailhead Diamond fragment ⅝" H. x ½" W. 1890–1900

Book A is a beautifully executed piece in a design frequently used by the Boston and Sandwich Glass Company. Three edges are concave to form pages. Book B was dug at the Boston and Sandwich site. Book C is from the family of James Lloyd. The glass lacks brilliance and does not fluoresce under a black light. It has the same color of documented glass from the Sandwich Co-operative Glass Company, in which Lloyd figured prominently. The design was cut with little skill and is similar to other pieces attributed to this company. Book D was also dug at the Boston and Sandwich site. Its design was in vogue after the close of the Boston and Sandwich Glass Company, so we attribute it to N. Packwood and Company. They rented the cutting shop until 1900.

3371 CUT OVERLAY TOY BOOK FRAGMENTS
(a) Alternate Block Diamond ⅝" H. x ½" W.
(b) Octagon Diamond 1" H. x ¾" W. 1870–1887

The penny clearly shows the size of such books. Book A would be completely covered if the penny were placed on top. Watch for toy books in display cases at antiques shows. They are often marked "samples", although we have not been able to document their commercial sale in any of the catalogs we have studied from cutting shops in the East or Midwest. The books are intricately cut on one cover. The other cover is cut in a simple design like photo 3366. Note the single diagonal lines cut through every other Block Diamond in Book A. When two parallel diagonal lines are made, they cut through the corners of the Block Diamonds, resulting in the Octagon Diamonds of Book B. Both were dug at the Boston and Sandwich Glass Company site.

THE CREATIONS OF NICHOLAS LUTZ DURING HIS YEARS AT SANDWICH

1870–1892

Nicholas J. Lutz stands high among the names of those who helped make Sandwich glass famous. He was responsible for bringing to the American glass industry several techniques that originated in Europe. Using skills he had acquired in France, he led the way in the design and manufacture of paperweights, striped glass and threaded glass. He encased ribbons of colored glass in clear glass rods and found ways to assemble them into lamps and tableware. He combined small amounts of colored glass with large amounts of clear glass in ingenious ways, and thus made it possible for the Boston and Sandwich Glass Company to compete inexpensively and profitably in the art glass market. He also developed methods for mass producing his work, making it possible for today's collector to find excellent examples of Sandwich glass made by Lutz and the men he trained.

Lutz was born to Nicholas and Ursula Lutz in Munzthal-Saint Louis, France, on February 21, 1835. His father was a skilled glass blower, like many of his relatives. Young Nicholas was apprenticed in 1845, at the age of ten, to the Cristalleries de Saint-Louis. Seven years later, he completed his apprenticeship and served the four years in military service required by the French government. At the age of twenty-one he returned to Saint Louis to improve his skills in making blown tableware and paperweights. Toward the end of 1860, production of paperweights had peaked in Europe. Now twenty-five, Lutz and six other glassworkers immigrated to New York City. Early in 1861 he began to work for Christian Dorflinger in Brooklyn.

Dorflinger had left the Saint Louis factory in 1846. After working in Philadelphia, Pennsylvania, and Camden, New Jersey, he established the Long Island Flint Glass Works in Brooklyn in 1852. He went on to establish two more factories in Brooklyn, one on Plymouth Street in 1858, and a third on Commercial Street in 1860. This last venture was the Greenpoint glassworks, noted for making Dorflinger's finest glass, and this is where Lutz was employed. Dorflinger himself left Brooklyn in 1863, planning to retire near White Mills, Pennsylvania. But by late 1865, he was hard at work in a new facility in White Mills. He moved experienced workers, including Nicholas Lutz, to

White Mills from his Brooklyn plants. By this time Lutz had expanded his area of expertise and was making other types of glass, such as stemware, finger bowls and inkwells. In the spring of 1867, he completed his employment with Christian Dorflinger and moved to the Boston area to work at the New England Glass Company in Cambridge.

Lutz brought with him the skills that allowed the New England Glass Company to engage successfully in the

Nicholas Lutz, head gaffer. *Courtesy, Sandwich Glass Museum, Sandwich Historical Society*

Frank Lutz
(glassmaker at B & S)
b. 1832
d. Mar. 3, 1872

m.

Annie ———

Nicholas F. Lutz
(glass blower at B & S)
b. 1860
d. Jan. 6, 1926

Frank Lutz
(sticker-up boy at B & S)
b. Dec. 17, 1871

m.

Catherine Elizabeth Miller

Joseph Lutz
b. Oct. 1, 1873
d. Jan. 1920

Frederick N. Lutz
b. Nov. 18, 1875
d. Feb. 14, 1880

Nicholas J. Lutz
(glass blower at B & S)
b. Feb. 21, 1835
d. Mar. 31, 1906

Mary Ursula Lutz
b. Jan. 7, 1878
d. Mar. 17, 1880

m. Sept. 10, 1870

Alphonsa Lutz
b. July 24, 1881
d. July 9, 1883

Elizabeth (Lizzie) Miller
b. Aug. 4, 1854
d. Dec. 23, 1939

Lewis Lutz
b. Nov. 7, 1883

Nicholas Lutz
(glass blower in France)

m.

Ursula ———
b. 1818
d. Feb. 4, 1903

Bertha U. Lutz
b. Feb. 22, 1886

Victor Ernest Lutz
(spokesman for the family)
b. Jan. 8, 1891
d. Sept. 25, 1967

Ursula Lutz
b. 1892
d. Oct. 29, 1973

William Edmund Lutz
b. June 11, 1893
d. Aug. 29, 1979

m. Mar. 4, 1923

Mary Ellen Fay
b. Aug. 31, 1897

Nicholas Smith
(glass cutter at Packwood)
b. 1868
d. 1949

Frank Smith
b. Sept. 23, 1871
d. Apr. 25, 1941

Mary Bridget Lutz
b. 1846
d. 1933

m. Dec. 25, 1893

Doris Zuleme Smith
(Sandwich Glass Museum Director)
b. June 16, 1902
d. Oct. 27, 1974

m. Sept. 1866

Zuleme Estelle Fish
b. Oct. 2, 1875
d. Apr. 25, 1942

m. Oct. 2, 1926

William Smith
(glass cutter at B & S, Packwood)
b. William Smidt, May 1846
d. Mar. 21, 1916

Joseph Robert Kershaw
b. 1894
d. Mar. 14, 1959

Mary J. Smith
b. Jan. 15, 1874

m. 1898

George T. Shepardson
(glass cutter)

LUTZ FAMILY GENEALOGY

Ten other children
(five died in infancy)

paperweight market. When the need for weights slackened, he made other articles that were part of the regular production run. During this time, he met Elizabeth (Lizzie) Miller, who later became his wife. His drive, however, to use his other glassmaking talents compelled him to leave the New England Glass Company in 1869.

Lutz spent the winter of 1869–1870 in Pittsburgh. While he was there, he wrote to the Phoenix Glass Works in South Boston to apply for a position. Phoenix made plans to hire him, but backed out of their agreement, citing a change of plans. In a letter dated March 29, 1870, the Phoenix Glass Works agent informed Lutz that if he came to Phoenix, they could use him only until the 16th of May.[1] If Lutz did indeed work at Phoenix (and there is no sure evidence he did), it was only for this short period of time. He married Lizzie Miller on September 10, 1870, and moved to Sandwich shortly thereafter to become a head gaffer at the Boston and Sandwich Glass Company.

Glassmaker families were closely-knit, and often went to great lengths to stay together. Nicholas' brother Frank was a glassmaker in Sandwich at the time of his death at the age of thirty-nine on March 3, 1872. Frank's teenage son, Nicholas F. Lutz, moved in with his Uncle Nicholas and Aunt Lizzie, who by this time had a son Frank, who

was born in Sandwich on December 17, 1871. Young Nicholas also became a glassblower at the Boston and Sandwich Glass Company. From time to time, he was listed in newspapers and union records as "Nicholas Lutz II" and "Nicholas Lutz, the younger of that name". To further complicate matters, young Frank became a sticker-up boy in the shop where his father was the gaffer, James Grady was the servitor, and William McQue[2] was assistant to the servitor. The children's grandmother, Ursula Lutz, also emigrated from Saint Louis and lived in the household. A sister, Mary Bridget, also came from France, and in September 1866, had married William Smith (William Smidt), a Sandwich glass cutter.

The birth of Nicholas and Lizzie's second son Joseph, on October 1, 1873, prompted the Lutz family to buy a house on State Street.[3] Nicholas was now employed by a company that allowed him the freedom to work at his trade as he saw fit. He could try new things in glassmaking, experiment with different colors, fabricate new molds for making more complex rods, and improve his skills to heights he had not reached before. By the 1870's, the company had grown to six hundred men and boys. As head gaffer, Lutz at last found complete happiness and a place to call "home".

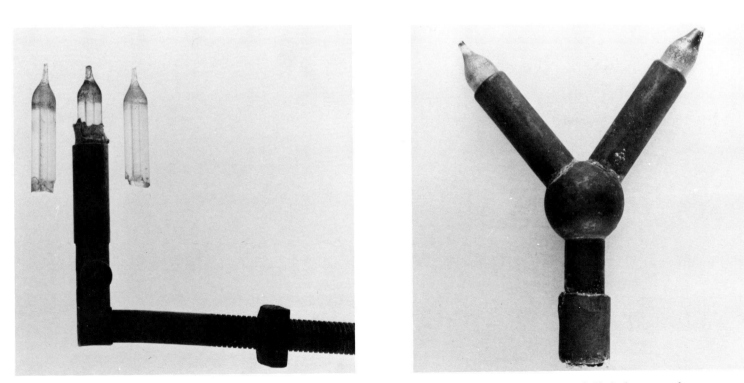

Gas burners used by Lutz in his Sandwich home for lampwork. The little glass tubes are each little burners that were fired by gas piped to his workbench. They were used to heat the glass rods to make flowers for paperweights. The ends of the tubes are seared as a result of the flame and the heat that the work generated. The burner on the left has a valve to control the flow of gas. The nut threaded onto the pipe was used to fasten the burner to the bench. The Y-shaped burner on the right carried two flames. All three flames burned at the same time. A jet of compressed air stretched the flame so that it burned a maximum amount of oxygen, giving an excellent heat source for working the glass. These burners were salvaged from Lutz's workbench and are now in the collection of the authors.

The house on State Street had gas piped into it, so Lutz made a work area in his cellar so that he could do *lampwork* during the hours he was not at the factory. Two small gas burners were attached to his workbench, supplying the heat he needed to make fruit, petals and leaves for paperweights by melting small amounts of glass taken from rods he had made at the factory. The petals and leaves were painstakingly assembled into flowers. Sometimes they did not meet the industry's standards, so Lutz discarded them. His bench had a hole in the center, large enough to take a completed weight. When an item he was working on did not come out the way he liked, down the hole it went into a drawer below. When the drawer was full, Lutz threw away its contents.

In addition to set-ups for paperweights, Lutz made writing pens from glass rods. These, too, were fabricated at home and then taken to the factory to add to his daily production. His reasons for conducting a "cottage industry" at home are not clear. Did he make flowers in the cellar because he enjoyed making them, or was he paid extra by the company? He often had fellow workers with him, teaching them how to make little glass finials, ducks, footballs. If the results were satisfactory, the pieces were retained by their makers, but if they were bad, they were thrown into the discard drawer.

It can be concluded, from an examination of Lutz's paperweight components and rods, that he worked mainly in red and blue combined with clear glass or opaque white. Perhaps his choice of color was influenced by love of country during the period of his becoming a citizen in 1876, which was also the year of America's Centennial.

A third son, Frederick N., was born on November 18, 1875, and a daughter, Mary Ursula, on January 7, 1878. They died within a month of each other in the spring of 1880.

In the late 1870's, a special machine was invented in England that could extrude a hot glob of glass into a thin continuous thread. The Boston and Sandwich Glass Company took immediate interest, and, toward the end of 1880, the factory was producing threaded glass in several colors (see Chapter 13, Volume 4). Pages from the 1887 factory sloar book, two of which appear at the end of the history portion of this chapter, show that much of the threading was done by Lutz's group.

He also made chandelier parts out of glass. The gaslight era created a need for elaborate lighting devices and gas shades. The company expanded its lighting operation in this field, so there was plenty of work for a highly skilled gaffer.

Lutz's young son, Frank, worked in his father's shop, and, after school on Saturdays, he and some of the other boys would return to the factory to pick up glass that had broken during manufacture. They sorted it into boxes according to color and were paid ten cents a box by the company.

The Lutz family was growing. A little girl, Alphonsa, was born on July 24, 1881. She lived less than two years, but was followed by Lewis, born November 7, 1883, and Bertha U., born February 22, 1886. Lutz sang tenor with a musical group in town. He also played a large part in the growth of the American Flint Glass Workers Union Local No. 16, to which his nephew, Nicholas F. Lutz, also belonged. The union, however, was prepared, perhaps unwittingly, to destroy everything Lutz had worked for. On November 27, 1887, it gave the glass company an ultimatum: improve working conditions and increase salaries or the union men would not return to work in the New Year (see Chapter 1 in Volume 4). On January 2, 1888, after the normal Christmas shutdown, the union lived up to its word. The fires remained blocked while workers and management waited out the stalemate in contract negotiations.

Lutz was sure the strike would not last, but he was able, at least, to supplement his income with outside work. Late in February, for example, he received a letter from a Pennsylvania glass house asking him to decorate ten thousand blown, opaque white, cigar holders. He agreed, and eleven thousand holders were sent to him to allow for error. They also sent matching boutonniere holders for men's lapels. With this volume of business conducted from his home, his family was able to remain in Sandwich and await the time when he would once again be employed at the factory. The younger Nicholas left Sandwich by June, but he was to return at a later time.

However, the Boston and Sandwich Glass Company did not reopen. The buildings were offered for sale in October 1888. Lutz's bench at home became a full-time operation. By the end of the year, he added the making of glass writing pens to his little cottage industry. He could no longer make rods at the factory, so he made arrangements with his relatives in France who were still employed at Cristalleries de Saint-Louis to export a quantity to Boston. The three-foot-long latticinio rods were shipped in bundles that were twelve to fourteen inches in diameter. The bundles were packaged in cylinders that were each placed in a box. Six boxes constituted one order. Lutz traveled to Boston to get them, and accompanied them on the train to Sandwich to make sure they did not break. The straight middle section of each rod was cut into pen handle lengths. The ends of each rod that were tapered (deliberately made this way to avoid breakage in shipping) were thrown down the discard slot in the workbench and into the drawer below. By adding a decorative finial to the handle, and a writing point fashioned from a slender reeded rod, Lutz had a salable item requiring minimal labor. He sold them through Jones, McDuffee and Stratton, a wholesale house in Boston.

The Boston and Sandwich Glass Company also sold its inventory to Jones, McDuffee and Stratton in the spring of 1889 (see page 19 in Volume 4). This inventory included all of the finished glass stored in the Boston warehouse and all glass, finished and unfinished, that was left in the still unsold factory in Sandwich. There were threaded wines and champagnes with no stems, and boxes of feet not yet attached. Jones, McDuffee and Stratton asked Lutz to complete the wines and champagnes by using the pen handle rods for stems. For the next several months, the Lutz boys carted boxes and barrels of glass from the factory to the house.

Lutz got other jobs from the wholesale house. He made

This photo was taken in Sandwich early in 1892, just before the Lutz family moved to New Bedford. From left to right are Nicholas, six-year-old Bertha, eighteen-year-old Joseph, eight-year-old Lewis, nephew Nicholas Lutz (also a glassworker), Elizabeth (Lizzie) holding one-year-old Victor, who was the last child to be born in Sandwich, twenty-year-old Frank, who was the oldest, and Ursula Lutz, the children's grandmother.

little glass hands that were wired to the arms of leather dolls and clock faces that were glued to toy grandfather clocks. Like so many of his co-workers, he found a way to make a living and stay in Sandwich for a while.

But financial needs became more and more demanding. He and Lizzie now had five children. Victor Ernest was born on January 8, 1891. Nicholas watched as the factory was sold to the Electrical Glass Corporation, which failed. He waited again as George B. Jones attempted to make glass — and failed. He finished decorating the last of the cigar holders, his inventory of stemware was depleted and the sale of writing pens became limited. In the spring of 1892, he decided to close down his business and take a position offered to him at the Mount Washington Glass Company in New Bedford.[4] He packed his belongings, including his workbench, his gas burners, and the one thousand extra cigar holders, decorated with little dots, that were in excess of the ten thousand needed by the Pennsylvania manufacturer.

The Lutz family settled down to life in New Bedford, where two more children were born, Ursula in 1892 and their last child, William Edmund, in 1893. But two years

after Nicholas started working in his new position, changes began to take place. On July 14, 1894, the Mount Washington Glass Company became part of the Pairpoint Manufacturing Company. Frederick Stacey Shirley, the guiding force behind Mount Washington's success, decided to try to revive the glass industry in Sandwich. He became part of a group associated with Albert V. Johnston that invested heavily in the Boston and Sandwich Glass Company II (see page 80 in Volume 4). Still owning his State Street house in Sandwich, Lutz invested his savings in the project[5] and put his Mount Washington job on the line. He was informed in no uncertain terms that if he left his position to return to Sandwich, his job would not be waiting for him if the Sandwich factory failed. The Boston and Sandwich Glass Company II began making glass in mid-1895, but by the end of 1896, the people of Sandwich witnessed another failure that brought financial disaster to many people, including the Lutz family.

By this time, Lutz had moved his family of seven children to Somerville, Massachusetts, and was working as a head gaffer at the Union Glass Company. He took the tools he needed at the factory, but left his home workbench

From time to time, Lutz's relatives sent examples of the work they did in France. The pieces were incorporated into the Lutz family collection. When these pieces entered the antiques market, the legend that every one was made by Nicholas Lutz became well established.

with its contents in the cellar at New Bedford. He had not used it because there was no gas piped into his New Bedford home. When lampwork was needed during the three years he was at Mount Washington, he did it at the factory. Lutz remained at the Union works until his death on March 31, 1906.[6] The small bench was forgotten, left to rot in the cellar.

HISTORY STORED IN A WORKBENCH

Our research into the work of Nicholas Lutz extended over a long period, from the time Doris (Smith) Kershaw, a granddaughter of Lutz's sister Mary, became the director of the Sandwich Historical Society in the 1940's, and Victor Ernest Lutz, son of Nicholas and spokesman for the family, disposed of the Lutz family's glass. We examined documents from many sources: Sandwich Archives and Historical Center, Sandwich Historical Society, Henry Ford Museum, and scrapbooks and records still in the care of Lutz family descendants. We were faced with the difficulty of segregating the glass made by Nicholas Lutz while he worked in Sandwich from the glass he made when he worked in France, Brooklyn, Pennsylvania, and other parts of Massachusetts. We had to evaluate his singular talent in order to be able to differentiate between Lutz family pieces that were made by Nicholas and pieces that were made by relatives in France. We had to deal with the "Lutz-type" glass made in Europe during the late 1800's,

as well as the never-ending problem of reproductions. As more and more factual information emerged, we were able to reach many conclusions. These were substantiated when the contents of Lutz's workbench became part of the Barlow collection in 1984.

As previously described, the bench was moved from Lutz's house in Sandwich to his home in New Bedford. Because gas was not available to him in New Bedford, he did not work at home. He lost interest in the bench. When he relocated again, the bench, with its drawer-full of rejected paperweight setups and tapered rod ends, was left in the New Bedford cellar. It remained there for over seventy-five years, until dampness took its toll. The legs rotted, the bench fell over and the drawer spilled out fragments that had been thrown into it *when Lutz was still in Sandwich.*

The drawer contained over five hundred sections of rods. There were over one thousand leaves, petals and fruit for paperweights. There were completed paperweights with defects that made them unsalable. There were writing pens, cigar holders, hands for leather dolls. There were birds, footballs and crosses that could be used in paperweights or as finials on pens. The list is long, and we must emphasize that these were not first-line items. They were all seconds (or worse) that were discarded by Lutz and the glassworkers that were tutored by him.

Lutz brought to Sandwich the techniques, but not the

skills, of the French masters. He left France when he was twenty-five years old. He gained experience over the next ten years, but at no time in his glassmaking career did he equal or surpass his French contemporaries. One need only to see a French paperweight side by side with an American one to know that the fledgling glass industry in the United States had a long way to go to equal work done in France. Lutz did not make great quantities of filigree (twisted) rods and ribbon rods that he fused together to make finger bowls, underplates, vases and pitchers. According to Victor Lutz, these very well made rods were sent to him from France. Nicholas incorporated them into writing pens and stemware. From time to time, family members sent examples of finished articles made from the same rods. These articles became Lutz family heirlooms, so over the years, as they were sold out of the family collection, the facts regarding their origin faded. Descendants living today have not retained pieces made from fused rods. Fragments have not been found at the Boston and Sandwich Glass Company dig site, and the 1887 sloar book pages preserved at the Sandwich Archives show that Lutz's workload consisted of a daily routine similar to other gaffers at the factory.

Nicholas Lutz excelled at combining a minimal amount of colored glass with a larger amount of clear glass to give the appearance of colored art glass.

He did this in one of four ways. The first was by encasing colored glass lampwork in clear glass to make paperweights. Most of the paperweights were flowers that resembled poinsettias. Some were pansies and other recognizable flowers, others were composed of imaginatively arranged petals having no botanical origin. The 1874 Boston and Sandwich Glass Company catalog simply lists *flower paperweights* and the 1887 sloar book lists *fancy weights*. It is the paperweight collector who gives them fanciful names. It is our opinion that the single complex cane in the center of the flowers was cut from imported rods that Nicholas rationed out very carefully. There are fruit weights, and some with colored leaves arranged into a flower form. Victor Lutz delighted in telling about his father working at home on the setups.

Secondly, threaded glass was made by him and/or under his direction. Most threaded glass was made by winding colored threads around the outside of thinly blown clear glass. Other gaffers to whom this work can be attributed worked in Lutz's shop. But there is, in our opinion, no difference between his work and the work of his assistants. Threaded glass should be attributed to Lutz's hand only with the strongest documentation.

Thirdly, Lutz made clear glass hollow ware, such as lamp fonts and wafer trays, with colored threads incorporated into the clear glass in a swirl configuration.

His fourth technique was similar, combining ribbons of colored glass in clear glass hollow ware to make swirled stripes. Striped glass has a larger proportion of color. Pieces made by Lutz that are all color were largely in the form of red, white and blue off-hand pieces such as epergnes, flasks or pipes. They were not part of the regular production line of the company.

Art glass that can be positively attributed to him was made when he was at the Mount Washington Glass Company and the Union Glass Company. According to Victor Lutz, in a letter dated January 31, 1955, Nicholas made a set of Burmese children's dishes for one of his daughters while he was still at Sandwich. He would only have been legally allowed to do this when he was helping Frederick S. Shirley establish the Boston and Sandwich Glass Company II in 1895.

The finding of Lutz's workbench should put to rest the use of the term *Lutz-type*, generally applied to glass made by fusing twisted filigree and ribbon canes side to side. Since there is no evidence that Nicholas Lutz made this type of glass, we do not have to deal with it at all, whether it be foreign or domestic, original or reproduction. In an article written for the Spring 1981 issue of *The Acorn*, Sandwich Glass Museum Director Barbara Bishop stated, " . . . there is no factual basis on which to say that any of the glass now called "Lutz-type" was made by Nicholas Lutz or under his direction." Regardless, Lutz has secured his place in history as a dedicated glassworker who devoted many hours to the service of his employer. His name will always be linked with Sandwich glass.

The paperweights and lampwork setups for paperweights that are shown in the following photos are those

Nicholas Lutz in his later years.

that we have traced back to Nicholas Lutz and can document without question. The Boston and Sandwich Glass Company made other paperweights, many "built" by the method employed by Lutz, some pressed and some cut. They are treated in a chapter devoted to Sandwich paperweights, and related items elsewhere in this series.

THESE SIMPLE HINTS WILL HELP YOU IDENTIFY SANDWICH GLASS MADE BY LUTZ.

Lutz used a small percentage of colored glass, predominantly red, white and blue, with a large percentage of clear glass.
Look for:

- Clear glass paperweights with colored lampwork.
- Threaded glass (threads applied after the piece was made).
- Colored threads incorporated into clear glass, swirled when the piece was being made.

- Striped glass (colored ribbons, sometimes alternating with threads, swirled when the piece was being made).

Learn the basic configuration of Lutz paperweights, i.e., a single flower with a complex cane center, a stem with two leaves, and an extra leaf or bud. You must have irrefutable documentation to attribute a particular weight to his years at Sandwich, because he used the same configuration at the New England Glass Company from 1867 to 1869.

All Lutz writing pens have slender reeded nibs. Lutz used only two types of rods—single color rods made at the Boston and Sandwich Glass Company before 1888, and imported latticinio rods. Both types of rods have a smooth surface.

Venetian-type tableware, made by fusing filigree and ribbon rods side to side, was not made by Lutz. This type of art glass was not made at Sandwich by anyone.

NOTES TO CHAPTER 11

1. Letter from the Phoenix Glass Works, addressed to Mr. Nicholas Lutz, Care F. T. South, Esq., Cor. 37th & Buttler Sts., Pittsburgh, Penn. It begins, "Since last we wrote you . . . " (Courtesy, Sandwich Glass Museum, Sandwich Historical Society).
2. As written in Lutz family documents. A William McHugh is listed as a glassworker in the 1880 Census.
3. Barnstable County (Massachusetts) Registry of Deeds, book 171, pages 72-73, dated October 9, 1873.
   According to *The Seaside Press*, a Sandwich newspaper dated October 25, 1873, Lutz purchased the homestead on State Street from the estate of Joseph Hobson. Hobson had been a glassworker.

4. *The Sandwich Observer* of July 19, 1892, stated that Mr. and Mrs. Nicholas Lutz of New Bedford were guests of William Smith. William Smith was a Sandwich glass cutter married to Nicholas' sister Mary.
5. Several original Boston and Sandwich Glass Company II documents were given to the Sandwich Glass Museum by the Lutz family. A list of Sandwich men on the payroll, dated after Frederick S. Shirley became general manager in 1896, does not include Lutz himself. It should not, because Lutz was an investor. (Courtesy, Sandwich Glass Museum, Sandwich Historical Society).
6. The death of Nicholas J. Lutz is recorded in the April 10, 1906, issue of *The Bourne Pioneer*.

3372 LAMPWORK FOR PAPERWEIGHTS
(a) Blue flower 1¼" across
(b) Blue and white striped flower 1¼" across
(c) Fruit forms ¼" Dia.
(d) Leaves ⅝"-¾" L.
(e) Flower buds and vegetable forms ½" L.
(f) Two red flowers 1¼"-1½" across 1870-1887

Realizing the historical value of their father's work, Lutz's descendants saw to it that the best of his effort was permanently preserved. These pieces may be seen at The Bennington Museum. Others are at the Sandwich Glass Museum. The leaves were shaped like petals. While each piece was still hot, Lutz placed it into a leaf-shaped squeeze mold. The two parts of the mold were in the jaws of pliers. The pattern of veins is only on the upper surface of each leaf; the back is flat. Some of Lutz's stems have red thorns applied to them. When the work on each tiny piece was completed, the leaves were attached to stems, the stems to flower petals, and the complete assembly was ready to be "built" into a paperweight. Once the setup was encapsulated by clear glass, it was a permanent part of the finished product. *The Bennington Museum, Bennington, Vermont*

3373 LAMPWORK FLOWERS FOR PAPERWEIGHTS
(a) Blue "weedflower" 1¼" across
(b) Red flower 1½" to bottom of stem 1870-1887

These intricate examples of Lutz's work clearly show his skill as a glassworker. The flowers are all made of glass. When placed in a weight, the curved surface magnifies the lampwork, making it look much larger. The blue flower is made up of eight parts: a cane center, five petals and two leaves. Flowers with striped petals are called *weedflowers* by collectors. The red flower is made up of nine parts: a center, five petals, a stem and two leaves, one of which has been broken off. Three of the petals and the center were made from a white rod that was cased with red. The rod was cut into thin slices, which were assembled as petals. Lutz was capable of making two-color rods, but not the complex cane used in the center of the blue flower. *Courtesy, Sandwich Glass Museum, Sandwich Historical Society*

3374 LAMPWORK FRUIT FOR PAPERWEIGHTS
¼"-⅞" L. 1870-1887

Fruit was used by Lutz at the New England Glass Company as well as at the Boston and Sandwich Glass Company. He made some of the fruit forms by pressing small globs of glass in a little mold, then reworking each molded piece into its final shape. Stems were hand formed and applied to the fruit by hand. The fruit was assembled, leaves were added, and the completed setup became the center of a paperweight.

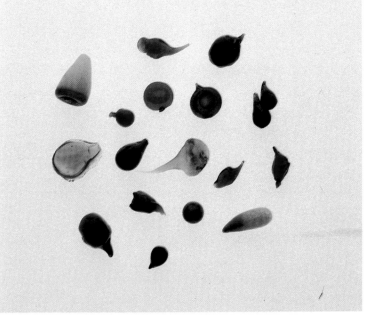

3375 RODS FROM LUTZ'S WORKBENCH
4"–9" L. 1870–1887

Every glass factory that made tableware was capable of producing simple rods. Thick ones were reheated to form handles that were applied to creamers, custards and molasses cans. Lutz made the thin rods shown here at the factory in Sandwich. He took them home to use for his lampwork. These pieces from the discard drawer in his bench are the tapered ends of the rods, left over after the straight usable portions were cut out. Some of the rods have white centers. They were cut into short segments and flattened out to form round flower petals with white centers, as shown in photo 3373. The rods when made were pulled like taffy until they were the required thickness, then cut into three foot lengths.

3376 LAMPWORK PETALS FOR FLOWERS
(a) Petals divided lengthwise
(b) Rod from which they were made 1870–1887

The rod is 50 percent red and 50 percent white. The petals were made by heating the end of the rod. When the rod softened, a small amount of glass was taken from the end of the rod, and was shaped into a petal. Lutz made sure each petal was divided by color lengthwise. If each petal was divided horizontally, only the color at the top of each petal would show in the finished assembly. The rod was made at the Boston and Sandwich Glass Company. Glass could not be made at Lutz's home, only reheated and reshaped.

3377 LAMPWORK PETALS FOR FLOWERS
1870–1887

We have shown you how the four red and white petals at the top of the photo were fashioned from a two-color rod. The single-color petals were made in the same manner from single-color rods. The larger petals were used in flowers that had only five or six petals. Lutz used smaller petals for flowers that had ten or more petals surrounded by leaves.

HOW LUTZ ASSEMBLED A SETUP FOR A FLOWER PAPERWEIGHT

3378

When we studied Nicholas Lutz's rejects, we realized that broken assemblies that were in the discard drawer could be reassembled to show you how a paperweight setup was made. The first step, after the individual units were formed, was to heat two petals and join them, using little dots of green glass, in the same manner that the Boston and Sandwich Glass Company used wafers of glass to join large units of tableware. Lutz's little "wafers" cannot be seen in the finished product.

3379

Here are assemblies to which Lutz added a third petal. Great care had to be taken in heating so that the shape of each petal would not be distorted. By applying a petal onto the little "wafer" rather than directly onto another petal, there was less chance of cracking the petals already assembled.

3380

Here are four-petal and five-petal assemblies. The flower is beginning to take shape. Lutz used the large flowers in 3½" Dia. weights and the small flowers in 2" Dia. weights. We seldom see a large weight made by Lutz that has several small flowers in it, although he often added a bud. Lutz reheated the dot in the center and applied a tiny section of cane.

HOW LUTZ ASSEMBLED A SETUP FOR A FLOWER PAPERWEIGHT (CONTINUED)

3381

Lutz completed these simple flowers, then added the leaves. At this point, they broke. They have been put back together, leaving the breaks visible so that you can see why he threw them away. It took a patient individual to make enough setups so that the company could include flower weights in their catalog as part of their regular production. One can be seen on page 42 of the 1874 catalog.

3382

Stem and leaf assemblies, made beforehand, were attached to the flower assemblies. An assortment of canes, bought by the Boston and Sandwich Glass Company from outside sources, were cut into thin segments and were applied to the center dot. The completed setup on the left has a center that was cut from a white over red hexagonal cane. The flower on the right has a white star-shaped cane with a red center. *The Bennington Museum, Bennington, Vermont*

3383

On the day when paperweights were to be made, Nicholas Lutz reportedly left his State Street home carrying dozens of setups ready to be encapsulated into "fancy weights". The center of the flower in this weight has eight points. The center canes in this weight and in the setups above, are simple, and may have been supplied by another glasshouse in the United States. *The Bennington Museum, Bennington, Vermont*

3384 FLOWER PAPERWEIGHT

1 ¾" H. after polishing; 2 ¾" Dia. 1870-1887

Although color variation can be seen in this grouping, sameness of form is apparent. A motif of two leaves on a flower with a cane center was repeated extensively, showing the mass production atmosphere prevalent at the Boston and Sandwich Glass Company during this period. Records show that on November 7, 1887, Lutz's shop made 150 such weights. There is some variation in the center cane, but these canes were made elsewhere. This weight has a complex cane made up of a predominantly white cane center surrounded by white and blue-green canes, most likely imported by the company from a French glass house. *Do not attempt to identify a Lutz weight by the center cane.* This weight was dug at the factory site, then polished so that we could study the flower, which had slipped to the side.

3385 FLOWER PAPERWEIGHT

1 ¾" H. x 2 ¾" Dia. 1870-1887

Lutz's paperweights are simple, straightforward and well-made, but lack imagination. Some of them have controlled bubbles strategically placed to look like dew drops. This flower is well-centered in the weight, but others are not. If they slipped slightly, they still maintained their salability. If they slipped badly, they were discarded. This flower has a cane with a rosette center surrounded by white and red. We describe the imported canes only to show their variety, not for identification. Our research places Lutz high on the "skilled" roster at Sandwich, but he was no competition to the French masters who made the complex center canes.

3386 FLOWER PAPERWEIGHT

1 ⅞" H. x 3 ¼" Dia. 1870-1887

Here is the same flower, the one most often referred to by collectors as a *poinsettia*. Its sameness is relieved only by a very complex center cane, made by surrounding a light blue and white cane with four red, white and blue canes that alternate with four white ones. The 1874 catalog lists *flower paperweights* without regard to their botanical name. The 1887 sloar book refers to *fancy weights*. What is a six-petalled flower? How many petals must it have to be called a clematis? At what point does a many-petalled clematis become a dahlia? Lutz didn't care—his shop mass produced pretty pieces to brighten a desk and hold down papers.

3387 FLOWER PAPERWEIGHT WITH LATTICINIO GROUND

2" H. x 2¾" Dia. 1870–1887

Lutz did not deviate much from his "basic model" configuration. Here is the familiar poinsettia varied by the placement of three large leaves behind it. But note its similarity to the paperweight below—the identical two-leaved stem on a latticinio ground. The flower center was made by surrounding a red, white and blue cane with alternating white and blue canes, bonded together by dark blue. Lutz must have regarded lampwork as a hobby in order to be able to devote to it so many hours.

3388 FLOWER PAPERWEIGHT WITH LATTICINIO GROUND

1¾" H. x 2⅝" Dia. 1870–1887

The petals on this flower were made by pressing yellow, pink, blue and green glass into the little mold that Lutz used to form leaves. A red and white star-shaped cane forms the center. This weight was among the contents of Lutz's workbench. It was unsalable because, when the clear glass cap was put over the flower, a streak of milky-colored gall (residue on the surface of hot glass in the pot) was deposited over the yellow petal. It would have been a beautiful weight. Unfortunately, weights could easily be spoiled. This particular paperweight was made in Sandwich, but Lutz also made them when he was at the New England Glass Company from 1867 to 1869. Any of the weights shown in this chapter may be found either with a latticinio or colored ground.

3389 FLOWER PAPERWEIGHT WITH SEPARATED SETUP

1½" H. x 2⅜" Dia. 1870–1887

Not every weight came out the way its maker wanted it to. This is what happened when the gaffer hesitated as he was positioning the hot cap of glass over the setup. The hot glass must completely surround the setup instantly. If there is hesitation for even a fraction of a second, the setup will break apart and the separated units will slide around. The red glass is the center of the flower. The striped petals were originally placed around the center to make a clematis-like flower, called a *striped flower* by collectors. It has also been found with a center that looks like a tiny rose.

3390 FLOWER PAPERWEIGHT

1¾" H. x 2⅞" Dia. 1870–1887

Here is a perfect paperweight that Nicholas Lutz was undoubtedly proud of. The petals were individually placed in perfect position, and the leaves were positioned properly on the stem. The complex cane was applied in the exact center of the flower. It was made by fusing together a red, white and blue cane surrounded by two concentric rings of blue and amber canes. A bud can be seen peeking out from behind the striped flower, replacing the third leaf in the weight shown previously.

3391 FLOWER PAPERWEIGHT

1¼" H. x 2⅞" Dia. 1870–1887

This pansy-like flower slid to the left. Study the flower and you will see that the red glass in the top petals overheated and ran as a result of the movement of the setup. This type of flower, with several striped petals, is called a *weed-flower* by some collectors. It has been found in other color combinations and may be on a latticinio ground. The center of this flower is made from a complex cane purchased elsewhere. Many white canes are encased in red, and there is a goldstone center. Lutz added a third leaf behind the flower and controlled "dew drop" bubbles. *The Bennington Museum, Bennington, Vermont*

3392 FRUIT PAPERWEIGHT WITH LATTICINIO GROUND

1⅝" H. x 2⅜" Dia. 1870–1887

Setups for fruit and vegetable paperweights were assembled in the same manner as petals for flowers. Each fruit or vegetable unit radiated from the center. This weight has four pears alternating with four small cherries or radishes. Another large pear is in the center. The same leaves that were used on flowers protrude from beneath the fruit. This weight was also made by Lutz when he was at the New England Glass Company, where it continued to be made after Lutz left. The New England version has more fruit, brighter colored glass and more clarity to the transparent glass. No Sandwich fruit weight has been found that contains more than five large fruit units.

3393 LATE-BLOWN VASES WITH PAPERWEIGHT BASE

(a) 7¾" H. x 4" Dia.
(b) 7⅞" H. x 4⅛" Dia. 1870–1887

Documentation from the Lutz family and The Bennington Museum reveals that Nicholas made this pair of vases for his wife, Lizzie. The workmanship lacks the detail and exactness of French pieces, yet the vases were made many years after Lutz's apprenticeship. From a Sandwich standpoint, they are more than acceptable, but below the standards set by the glass industry for this time period. Pink, blue and yellow bits of glass were formed into apples, pears and vegetables. Green leaves were added, and the base was "built up" into a paperweight. A spool stem and blown upper unit completed each vase. Museum records state that they were intended for cutting. There were several glass cutters in the Lutz family. *The Bennington Museum, Bennington, Vermont*

3394 BLOWN LAMP WITH TWISTED RIBBON STANDARD

9½" H. x 4½" Dia. 1876

Once again we see Nicholas Lutz's application of red, white and blue in the twisted ribbon rod that he used for the standard of this kerosene lamp. Just above the rod, a wafer holds the standard to the knop that forms the font extension. A second wafer below the rod holds the standard to the knop that is part of the base. The lamp was one of the pieces made for Elizabeth (Lizzie) Lutz both to commemorate Lutz's citizenship and the country's centennial. This piece is documented beyond doubt, but do not make the mistake of believing that every Lutz piece using these colors was made for the Centennial. Lutz produced many pieces with twisted ribbon standards when he worked at the Union Glass Company in Somerville. *The Bennington Museum, Bennington, Vermont*

3395 LETTER SEAL HANDLE WITH PAPERWEIGHT KNOB AND TWISTED RIBBON SHANK

2⅞" H. x 1⅛" Dia. 1870–1887

This piece is from the family of glass engraver John B. Vodon. Vodon worked at the Boston and Sandwich Glass Company and later established his own cutting and engraving shop, where in 1895 he was polishing out pontil marks for the Boston and Sandwich Glass Company II. An initialled metal piece was slipped onto the square end of the shank and was used to impress sealing wax. We understand that, in later years, similar handles were made with a complete set of interchangeable initials. Lutz was capable of making the twisted ribbon rod used for the shank, but not the complex quatrefoil canes that are arranged in two concentric circles in the knob. The authors are not the first to speculate that the Boston and Sandwich Glass Company imported canes from Cristalleries de Baccarat.

3396 BLOWN PIPE
12¼" L. to broken mouthpiece; 2⅝" Dia. bowl
1870-1887
Pipes had no practical purpose. They were carried in parades and hung above fireplaces. Although they were not part of a company's regular production, we have seen an invoice for one, so not only glassworkers owned them. Without documentation, there is no way to tell where simple blown pieces were made. This pipe is in a Sandwich home. The design made by trailing threads into loops is called *marbrie*. For more information on this technique, see the marbrie witch balls in Chapter 8.

3397 BLOWN PIPE
19½" L.; 3⅛" Dia. bowl 1870-1887
Fragments of pipes dug at the factory site are red and white, blue and white, and red, white and blue. In her booklet *History of Sandwich Glass* published in 1925, Bangs Burgess stated that gaffer Lutz made her a pipe that held a pound of tobacco. The red and white fragment matches the red and white pipe in photo 3396.

3398 BLOWN FLASK
7" H. x 4¼" W. x 1¾" D. 1876
This flask was made by Nicholas Lutz, who used it at a celebration when he became an American citizen on October 13, 1876. Lutz's daughter Ursula remembered seeing it being used on several other special occasions. It was sold to the author by son Victor. This piece has enough documentation behind it so there is no doubt of its origin.

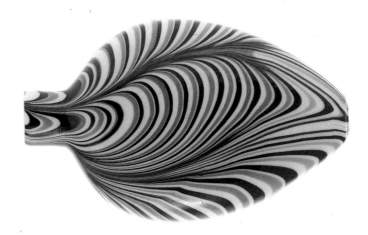

3399 BLOWN EPERGNE
20" H. x 10¼" Dia. 1876

This epergne again shows Lutz's use of red, white and blue. He made it for his family as a constant reminder that he became a citizen in the year of his adopted country's Centennial. The loops are similar to the loops on witch balls. The underside of the base and the inside of the trumpet and center bowl are cased in white. The bowl has a ruby rim. The base is held to the bottom of the bowl with a wafer. The trumpet is attached to the bowl with the same threaded fittings that the Boston and Sandwich Glass Company used on Onion lamps. Fruit was placed in the center bowl, and flowers were placed in the trumpet. *The Bennington Museum, Bennington, Vermont*

3400 BLOWN STRIPED CREAMER
4¼" H. 1870–1887

Striped glass is rarely found on the open market, so little is known about it. The fragments in the foreground are an exact match. Many fragments were dug at the Boston and Sandwich Glass Company in clear with blue and white, clear with pink and white, and clear with white. Matching rods that were used to make the handle were found in Lutz's workbench. The creamer was blown, then held by a pontil rod while the handle was attached. Study the way the gaffer applied the top of the handle to the body of the creamer. The upper end of the striped rod was flattened and spread out to give the handle strength. Then the rod was bent close to the body and was firmly attached at its lower end. This creamer was made for table use, not as a decorative "shelf piece". Do not buy a piece of hollow ware that has a crack radiating from the spot where the handle was applied. Unscrupulous dealers often try to sell broken pieces by saying that it cracked in the making. Glass factories did not sell broken dishes.

3401 BLOWN STRIPED TUMBLER
3⅛" H. x 2⅜" Dia. 1870–1887

Glassworkers often brought home "seconds". When we evaluate a worker's talent by examining his own collection, we must keep this constantly in mind. This tumbler has a pink stripe missing, with an extra white stripe in its place. Ruth Webb Lee shows another "second" from the Lutz collection on plate 23 in her book *Sandwich Glass*. Study the tumbler on the right of plate 23 and count the stripes from the bottom up. The first stripe is white, the second is colored, the third is white, the fourth is colored, the fifth is white, and the sixth *should be colored*, but it is not. We consider "seconds" more desirable because they have characteristics that make them one-of-a-kind. There is no question that striped glass was made in the shop headed by Lutz.

3402 BLOWN STRIPED WAFER TRAYS

(a) Red, white and clear 2¼" H. x 3⅛" Dia.
(b) Blue, white and clear 2" H. x 2½" Dia. 1870–1887
Nicholas Lutz, as head of a shop, worked in many ways.
These beautiful, delicate pieces are not toy compotes. They
are wafer trays, to hold the wafers that were used to seal
letters before the advent of envelopes. The letters were
folded, sealed, and the address was written on the back.
The Boston and Sandwich Glass Company also produced
striped inkwells. A matching wafer tray and inkwell made
a lovely set for a lady's desk. This type of glass is often
mistaken for Venetian work. Three of these were purchased from the Lutz family and are now in the authors'
collection. Over a dozen were available at the time. The
penny gives you an idea of their size.

3403 THREE-DOLPHIN LAMP WITH
CIRCULAR BASE AND BLOWN STRIPED FONT

11½" H. 1870–1887
The three-dolphin standard was made over a long period
of time. The brass fitting connecting the standard to the
font dates back to the beginning of the kerosene era. But
it is unlikely that striped glass was produced at the Boston
and Sandwich Glass Company before Lutz came in 1870.
This blown kerosene font is a combination of a blue stripe
alternating with white threads. Striped fonts are more
attractive when they are filled with kerosene because the
stripes do not reflect through from the opposite side. The
type of work shown in this chapter is as close as the Boston
and Sandwich Glass Company ever came to producing "art
glass".

3404 THREADED CREAMERS

(a) Plain 4" H. x 2½" Dia.
(b) Rigaree and needle etching 4" H. x 3¼" Dia.
    1880–1887
Threaded glass did not come to Sandwich until 1880, but
for seven years after it was heavily produced. It was well
liked by factory personnel and can be found in many
family collections. Pieces matching creamer A are in the
family collection of Henry F. Spurr, general manager of
the company. Creamer B is the same straight-sided shape
(called a *can*), but rigaree was applied over the threading.
The rigaree made it difficult to apply the handle, so it lacks
the pleasing form of the handle in A. The piece is clumsy
to handle and hard to store. Needle etching in the plain
area resembles Craquelle glass. See Chapter 13 in Volume
4 for more information about machine threading.

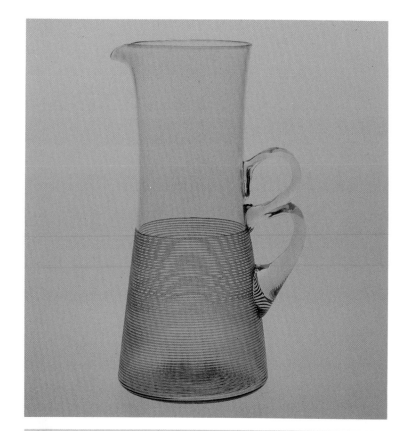

3405 THREADED DOUBLE-HANDLED TANKARD

10⅛" H. x 4⅝" Dia. 1880–1887

After Nicholas Lutz died, the bulk of the glass he had made for his family was left for Victor E. Lutz to dispose of, with the family's permission. Victor became the spokesman for the family, and helped to spread his father's fame throughout the collecting world. Victor made sure that the highest quality articles were made available to museums. According to Richard Carter Barret, former director-curator of The Bennington Museum, there are only two known examples of this tall double-handled tankard. Boston and Sandwich Glass Company pieces were machine threaded, using a method that originated in England in the late 1870's. *The Bennington Museum, Bennington, Vermont*

3406 THREADED PAPERWEIGHT

1¾" H. x 3⅛" Dia. 1880–1887

Here we see the use of threading that did not work. Ruby threads were arranged on the surface of a dome-shaped core of clear glass. To complete the weight, a clear glass cap was placed over the threads. The result was a disaster, so Lutz took it home. Families were often the recipients of failures. After all, this weight held down paper even if it did little to add to the decor of the desk. Some threaded weights did reach the market, but have more value as threaded curiosities than as paperweights. The black discoloration is the rough pontil mark on the base reflecting through the glass.

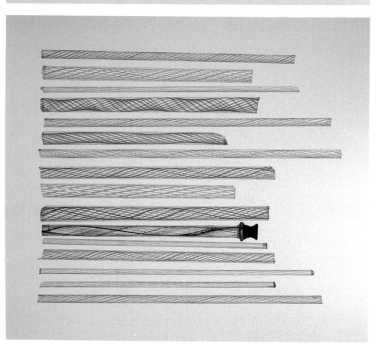

3407 LATTICINIO RODS FROM LUTZ'S WORKBENCH

¼"-⅝" Dia. 1888–1892

Rods with delicate threads running through them, either parallel or twisted, were not made in Sandwich. Nicholas Lutz did not have this talent. They were shipped from France by his glassworker relatives to aid him in the making of pens after the Boston and Sandwich Glass Company closed. Note the limited use of color, and the predominance of red and blue. Records show that the rods were 36" long. Lutz cut the straightest parts into pen-length sections. The pieces in this photo are the short tapered sections that were left over. Look at the sixth rod from the bottom. Lutz had begun the assembly and it broke. Keep in mind that all of the fragments left in his bench were accumulated during his Sandwich years.

3408, 3409, 3410 WRITING PENS MADE BY LUTZ

7½"–9⅝" L. 1870–1890

This fine collection of pens was assembled by Victor E. Lutz. They were purchased from him by The Bennington Museum, where they are on display, mounted to avoid breakage. The best, straightest pens were made when Lutz was at the factory, where he had better control of the gas burners for more accurate work. Most of the pens that were sold by the Boston and Sandwich Glass Company were made from solid color rods. After the factory closed, Lutz continued to make the same pens at home, but his supply of Sandwich rods ran short, so 1890 is a realistic approximation of the end of their production. All of the pens known to have been made by Lutz himself have long clear glass writing points. These nibs were made from the same type of reeded rods that were used to make reeded handles and claw feet on tableware, but were more slender. The reeds formed long grooves that held a surprisingly good supply of ink, allowing for continuous writing for several minutes. *The Bennington Museum, Bennington, Vermont*

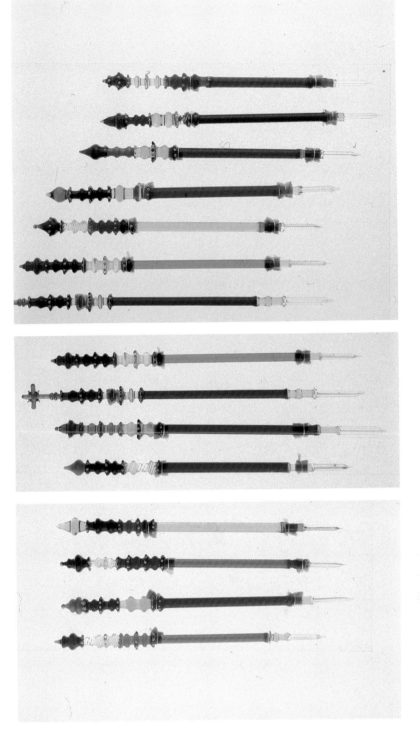

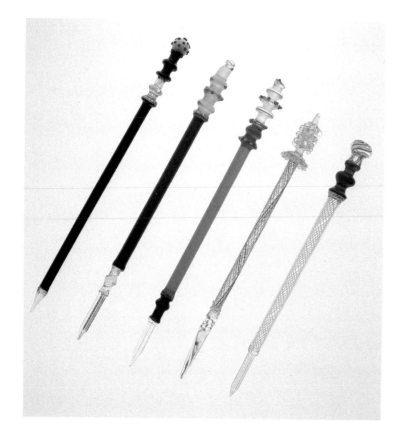

3411 WRITING PENS
(a) Short nib 1849–1855
(b) Slender reeded nib made by Lutz 1870–1890
(c) Slender reeded nib made by Lutz 1870–1890
(d) Twisted nib 1865–1870
(e) Slender reeded nib made by Lutz 1888–1892
    5¾"–6½" L.

The easiest way to date Sandwich pens is to examine the nibs (writing points). Pen A, at top, a perfect pen with red dots on the finial, has a short, smooth nib. This nib is the earliest, most primitive writing point that can be attributed to the Boston and Sandwich Glass Company. The short nib was improved by making grooves to hold the ink just above the taper, as shown in Fig. 16B below. Pens B and C were in Lutz's bench, discarded because the tops of the finials had broken. They have the slender reeded nibs perfected by Lutz, and were assembled from single-color rods produced by the Boston and Sandwich Glass Company. Pen D with the curly finial, broken at the top, has a long twisted nib that was used at the factory after the Civil War and before Lutz was employed there. The latticinio rod was purchased from an outside source. This twisted nib was a refinement over the earlier grooved nib, but it did not write as well as pen E, a perfect pen with a slender reeded nib, assembled by Lutz from a French latticinio rod.

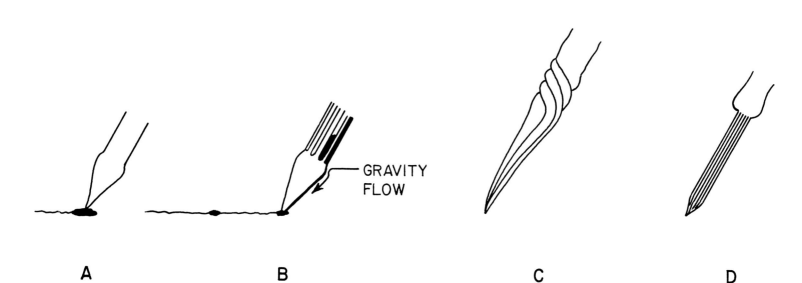

A　　　　　　　**B**　　　　　　　**C**　　　　　　　**D**

GRAVITY FLOW

Fig. 16　Nibs on Sandwich pens. Nib A is found on the earliest pens, made at the Boston and Sandwich Glass Company between 1849 and 1855. The nib is short, with no grooves to hold a supply of ink. It did not write well. The ink did not flow evenly and left large ink blobs on the paper. Only a word or two could be written. The short nib was improved in 1855 by adding grooves *above* the taper, shown on nib B. Writing time was increased, but the nib still left small blobs. Gravity released ink from one groove at a time, so the pen had to be rotated each time a groove was empty. This nib was employed until 1860. The Civil War temporarily halted the production of non-essential items. After the Civil War, reeded handles and claw feet came into style on Late Blown Ware. The reeded rods used to make the handles and claw feet were twisted to make nib C with its rounded ribs on a lengthened taper. When Lutz came to Sandwich in 1870, he pulled the reeded rods until they were thin, and did not twist them. This turned out to be the perfect solution. If you want pens assembled by Lutz, look for nib D with its straight reeded shaft ending in a fine tapered point.

3412 WRITING PEN FRAGMENTS FROM LUTZ'S WORKBENCH

1870-1892

Broken pen parts are a great help in identifying Lutz pens. The latticinio rods shown in photo 3407 can be seen in some of the partial assemblies. Lutz's slender reeded nib is in the center of the top row. Study the way it is fastened to the blue rod, a characteristic of Nicholas' work. Finials with latticinio canes were assembled after 1888. The red, white and clear striped glass finial on the right of the second row was made by Lutz at the factory prior to 1888. Red, white and blue are the dominant colors, even in assemblies that date into the 1890's. If you study the two types of rods used by Lutz, you will not make an error in identifying his work. The making of glass pens was revived in the 1920's, for use by savings banks as premiums when a new account was opened. Some are exquisite — birds with finely detailed eyes, beaks and wings.

3413 THREADED CHAMPAGNE WITH LAMPWORK STEM

5⅝" H. x 3½" Dia. with damaged stem
6⅜" H. x 3½" Dia. if perfect 1889

Jones, McDuffee and Stratton bought all of the leftover stock after the Boston and Sandwich Glass Company closed. There were boxes of champagnes and wines that were not complete. The tops were threaded and the feet were made, but there were no stems. Nicholas Lutz was asked to assemble them at home. He made the stems the same way he built up his pens. Jones, McDuffee and Stratton sold them from their Boston showroom. This piece is broken just below the threading. The Bennington Museum believes there should be another ¾" to balance that length at the bottom of the stem. *The Bennington Museum, Bennington, Vermont*

3414 BLOWN CIGAR HOLDERS DECORATED BY LUTZ

3"-3¼" L. 1888-1892

These cigar holders were not made in Sandwich. Eleven thousand of them were sent to Lutz to be *decorated* at his home. He was to complete an order for ten thousand and was allowed the extra ones for breakage. Lutz's only overhead for this job was labor. Leftover tapered ends of rods could be melted down to make designs out of dots. The holders were to be given away by cigar stores, along with boutonniere holders. The affidavit signed by Nicholas' son Victor indicates that Lutz made them for cigarettes. Victor, born in Sandwich in 1891, had no way of knowing that his father did not *make* them. A letter from Alice Montague Kelleher, sister-in-law of Sandwich glassworker Thomas Kelleher, states that Thomas told her the holders were for small *cigars*. The rims were crimped to prevent the holders from rolling off the table. Look for them at flea markets. Some have deer on them, and some have evergreen trees, made from little dots.

135 Antrim Street,
Cambridge 39, Mass.

I hereby guarantee that this cigarette holder was made by my father, Nicholas Lutz, in Sandwich prior to the close of the Boston & Sandwich Glass Co. in 1888.

Victor E. Lutz

3415 BLOWN BOUTONNIERE HOLDER

2¼" L. x ¾" Dia. at rim; ⅜" Dia. of tube 1888–1892
Not made in Sandwich, this flower holder for a man's lapel
was produced by a Pennsylvania glass house to match the
cigar holder. The Lutz family remembers that Nicholas
often used one in his lapel for flowers that he grew in his
garden. A small amount of water placed in the holder kept
the boutonniere fresh. This holder is still in the Lutz
family collection.

3416 LAMPWORK FROM LUTZ'S WORKBENCH

1870–1892
Nicholas Lutz's bench had some interesting things in it.
At the top of this photo is part of a cross, used in paperweights dating back to 1870, and as the finial for writing
pens. A football, the face of a toy clock and a bird are in
the center row. The bird has blue eyes and a yellow beak.
The hands were made for the arms of leather dolls. If they
weren't formed correctly so they could be wired onto the
doll, they were discarded. The left one has only a thumb.
Lutz made the clock faces and hands for Jones, McDuffee
and Stratton, a wholesale house that distributed the finished toys. These artifacts do not represent Lutz's talent.
Remember that they were discards, and some of them
may have been made by glassworkers he was teaching.

3417 LAMPWORK FROM LUTZ'S WORKBENCH

1870–1892
Many of the pieces were poorly made. We learned that
Lutz taught young men who visited his home. This would
explain the lack of quality. Most of the letters were too
large to become part of a Sandwich paperweight, but
might have been the forerunners for the larger weights
made at the Union Glass Company in Somerville, Massachusetts. Chains were a challenging exercise because it was
difficult to keep the links from adhering to each other. The
military bars, flags, and shields reflect Lutz's passion for
red, white and blue. We may never know what many of
the items in his bench were intended for.

1887   **Nicholas Lutz**

N. Move	Articles	N. made	Loss	packed	
7	Ink wells for Stone	4	made wrong	1	1 on hand
	lerner rd to patt	2+2			
8	5/ Bowls to patt R.C.	103	3 broken	100	
9	5 in 5/Gls offr	155	2 "	16—153	
10	Cov 5/Gls to patt G/S	73	3 " 1 had †	5—3	
	" " " B/S	311		3—2 27	
			Aug 29th		
1	Har B Bottls	138	3 crooked 2 chipp	133	2 on hand
2	Mustds + Cor	23+21	1 broken 1 Bnk	20. 20	
	Tumbs to patt	44		44	
	S/B "	16		16	
3	1 Cor for Box	1		1	
	Laps to patt	154			
4	Inks "	115	8 broken	287	
5	" "	180			
6	Glo Mustds	78		78	
	st "	67		67	
7	Linng to for frame	3		2	1 "
	Ink wells 2 sizes	4		2	2 "
	Tums to patt	2		1	1 "
	" "	12	1 broke	11	
	1/3 pr Lgr S to patt	17		17	
	Inks to patt	57	2 bad	55	
	Linng to for frame Blue	4	2 broken	2	
	Shade to patt	6		6	
8	1/2 pr Catsup Bottls	125	2 bad	141	
9	" "	18			
	3 Litr Glo hune Oils	129	1 crooked		
10	Clarets to patt	79	3 broke 1 bad	76	
	5 in 5/Gls offr	28	1 flew	27	
			Sept 5th		
1	Goblets to patt	126	2 bad chipp 1 flew	123	
2	Lgr Spere Bur	159+1	4 " "		
	Tumbls to patt	20	1 "	19	
3	1/2 pr Lgr h Oils	127	6 crooked in W		
4	" Catsup Bottls	123	3 bad made		
5	Mustard Lins	84		84	
	Sene S to patt	14		14	
	Cover "	2			
	Rods 35 in Long 3/4 dia	5		2	3 on hand
	Fessenden Goblts	36	1 crooked 2 cord	33	
6	Clarets to patt	142	5 broken 1 "	136	
7	1/2 pr Glo h Oils	152	8 crooked		
8	13 " S to patt +10	188	1 Bad	183	

Page 57 of the Boston and Sandwich Glass Company sloar book. Nicholas Lutz's shop was required to make ten moves each week. The top of the page is a continuation of the week of August 22, 1887. For the eighth move, the shop made 103 finger bowls with ruby threads. Three were broken and one hundred were packed. For move ten, Lutz made seventy-three covers for 5" Dia. finger bowls with green threads and thirty covers with blue threads. Today a covered piece would not be recognized as a finger bowl. Part of move five for the week of September 5 was five 35" L. x ¾" Dia. rods. Two were packed and three were kept for their own use. Seventeen pages record Lutz's work from May 31, 1887, to the end of the year. *Sandwich Archives and Historical Center*

1887 — *Nicholas Lutz*

No. more	Articles	No. Made	Loss	Packed	
6	Stopper to patt	2		1	1 on hand
	F/4 " "	2		1	1 "
	Sml Ale hrh to patt	33		33	
7	" " "	116	11 specks	95	
8	Bottles to patt	83	2 broken	81	
	Rnd Ale hrhs	21	3 " 5 specks	13	
	Deep Custards	26	1 broken hand	25	
9	Gill hand Oils	291	4 "	287	
10	Low ft finger bowls *purple*	24	1 Bad	23	
	6in Fish globes off ft	107	(3 flew)	104	

Oct 31st

1	Goblets to patt	81	2 bad 2 bro	77	
	Tipper "	4		4	
	Linings to for metal	10	1 broken	9	
2	Oval Bot Plaster	2		1	1 on hand
	Inks & Lazis	61		61	
	Vinegars for Stands	28-29		28-29	
	4½ Mav. Cluster	18		18	
3	" " "	13	2 broke	11	
	Bell Shape Glass	30		30	
	Vacuum Glass	1		1	
	Jar Covs to Sample	2	1 bro	1	
	Lining to for frames	8		6	2 on hand
	Box to for Cov	2		1	1 "
	Lining to for frame *Blue*	2	will not fit		
4	Low ft finger bowls *purple*	136		136	
5	" " "	142	11 broken		
6	Saucer Champ to patt	137	1 bad 3 broke	133	
7	U.C. F bowls to patt	114	1 " 3 "	110	
	Blue Lining for pan	2		2	
	Flint " "	2		2	
8	100/3 Hot Whiskers	140	4 crooked 1 broke	135	
9	4½ inks 1 "	6		6	
	5" hard Whistles	40-9		40-9	
	1st "	48-9	1 broke 1 Bad	46-9	

Nov 7th

1	Fancy P Weights	150	2 broke	148	
2	" "	44	1 "	43	
	For S to patt	42		42	
	Stopper "	2		1	1 on hand
	Lilys	92		92	

Page 61 of the Boston and Sandwich Glass Company sloar book. The notations can be deciphered with careful study. Move ten for the week of October 24, 1887, consisted of twenty-four purple low foot finger bowls and 107 6" Dia. fish globes "off feet". One finger bowl was bad, leaving twenty-three to be packed. Three fish globes flew (shattered in the annealing leer) and 104 were packed. The shop began the week of November 7 by making 150 fancy paperweights, two of which broke. Note the number of plain linings that were made to fit metal frames. Because they have no pattern, they cannot be identified as Sandwich glass today unless you know the company that made the frame and have invoices showing the linings were ordered from the Boston and Sandwich Glass Company. *Sandwich Archives and Historical Center*

GLOSSARY

ADVENTURINE See *goldstone*.

ANNEAL The gradual reheating and slow cooling of an article in a leer—an oven built for the purpose. This procedure removes any stress that may have built up in the glass during its manufacture.

APPLIED The fastening of a separate piece of glass, such as a base, handle, prunt, or stem, to an article already formed.

BATCH Mixture of sand, cullet, and various raw materials that are placed in the pot to be heated into metal, or molten glass.

BLANK A finished piece of glass requiring additional work, such as decorating or engraving.

BLOWN GLASS Glass made by the use of a blowpipe and air pressure sufficient to give it form.

BLOWN MOLDED GLASS Glass made by blowing hot glass into a plain or patterned mold, and forcing it with air pressure to conform to the shape of the mold.

BOX A container of any shape and any size. It can be square, rectangular, circular or oval.

BUTTON STEM A connector between the base and the body of any article, with a button-shaped extrusion in its center.

CANE In *paperweight making*, a bundle of various colored rods that are arranged into a design, fused by reheating, pulled until it is long and thin, cooled and then cut into segments.

CASING A different colored layer of glass, either on the inside or outside of the main body of a piece.

CASTOR PLACE The location in the factory where glass was cast (pressed) into molds.

CLAW FOOT An applied reeded foot resembling a scallop shell.

CLUSTER On *cut glass*, a grouping of similar designs in close proximity.

CRAQUELLE Glass that has been deliberately fractured after it has been formed, and reheated to seal the fractures, leaving the scars as a permanent design.

CROSSCUT DIAMOND On *cut glass*, a diamond that is divided into quarters.

CULLET Glass made in the factory and saved from a pot to be used in making future batches. Also, glass items already annealed; either produced in the factory or purchased, and broken to be included in future batches.

CUTTING The grinding away of a portion of the surface of a blank, using wheels and wet sand, to produce a design.

DECORATING The ornamenting of a blank by painting or staining it with a non-glass substance.

DESIGN The ornamentation of glass after it has been annealed, by cutting, engraving, etching or decorating.

DONUT On *Trevaise*, the wafer-size glob of glass applied to the base. In most cases, the center of the wafer is dished out, leaving the shape of a donut.

ENGRAVING The process of cutting shallow designs and letters into a blank using copper wheels and an abrasive.

ETCHING An inexpensive method of producing a design by using hydrofluoric acid to eat into the surface of a blank.

FILIGREE ROD A rod that has spiral or straight threads running through it. Also called *latticinio*.

FINIAL The decorative, terminal part of a newel post, writing pen, etc. The part of a cover used as a handle.

FIRE POLISHING Reheating a finished piece to remove marks left by tools or molds, leaving the article with a smooth surface.

FLASHED On *cut glass*, a fan-like design located between the points of a fan, hobstar, or star.

FLINT GLASS Glass made from metal containing lead. In the 1800's, the factory term for clear glass.

FLOATED In *decorated opal glass*, the method used to apply a solid color background.

FLUTE The hand-crimping of a rim. On *pressed* or *cut glass*, a panel rounded at the top.

FOLDED RIM A rim on either the body or base of a piece, the edge of which is doubled back onto itself, resulting in greater strength.

FRAGMENTS Broken pieces of finished glass, discarded at the time of production.

FREE-BLOWN GLASS Glass made by blowing hot glass and shaping it into its final form by the use of hand tools.

GAFFER In a group of glassworkers, called a *shop*, the most skilled artisan; the master glass blower.

GATHER The mass of hot metal that has been gathered on the end of a blowpipe.

GATHERER The assistant to the master glass blower, who gathers the hot metal on the end of the blowpipe.

GAUFFER To crimp or flute.

GILDING The application of gold for decorative purposes.

GLASS GALL Impurities skimmed from the surface of melted glass. Also called *sandever*, *sandiver*.

GOLDSTONE Glass combined with copper filings.

HOBSTAR On *cut glass*, a many-pointed geometrically cut star.

KNOP A round knob, either hollow or solid, in the center of a stem.

LAMPWORK The making and assembly of leaves, petals, stems, fruit and other small parts from rods of glass that have been softened by heating them over a gas burner. Originally, oil lamps produced the open flame.

LAPIDARY STOPPER A cut, faceted stopper.

LATTICINIO A rod of glass or a paperweight background composed of threads arranged in lattice, spiral or swirl configurations. The threads are usually white.

LEER A tunnel-shaped oven through which glass articles are drawn after formation for the purpose of annealing. Also spelled *lear*, *lehr*.

MAKE-DO A damaged item that has been repaired to "make it do" what was originally intended.

MARBRIE In *blown glass*, a loop design made by looping and trailing threads of glass through another color, such as in paperweights and witch balls.

MARVER Iron plate on which hot glass is first shaped by rolling, in preparation for blowing into its final form.

MERESE A wafer-shaped piece of hot glass, used to connect individual units to make a complete piece, such as the base and socket of a candlestick or the bowl and standard of a footed nappie.

METAL Glass either in a molten condition in the pot, or in a cold, hardened state.

MOLD A form into which glass is blown or pressed to give it shape and pattern. Also spelled *mould*.

MOLD MARKS On glass that has been blown or pressed into a mold, the marks or seam lines left by the edges of the units of the mold.

MOVE A period of time during which a shop makes glass continuously. A glass blower is expected to make ten *moves* each week.

NAPPIE A shallow bowl of any size, whether round bottomed or flat bottomed, which can be on a standard. Also spelled *nappy*.

NEEDLE ETCHING Done by coating a blank with an acid-resisting substance, then inscribing a design into the resist with a sharp needle. The blank is then dipped into hydrofluoric acid, which etches the glass where the design was inscribed.

NIB The writing point of a pen.

OVERFILL On pieces that have been blown or pressed into a mold, the excess hot glass that seeps into the seams of the mold.

PANEL A section with raised margins and square corners.

PATTERN (ON GLASS) The specific ornamentation into which *hot* glass is formed.

PATTERN (WOODEN) Wooden model carved in detail that is sent to the foundry, used as a guide to shape a mold.

PEG On a *lamp*, the unit that holds the oil and is attached to the base with a metal connector.

PICKWICK A pointed instrument for picking up the wick of a whale oil or fluid lamp.

PILLAR-MOLDED GLASS Glass made by first blowing a hot gather of glass into a mold with vertical ridges (pillars). A second cooler gather is blown into the first. The hot outer layer conforms to the shape of the mold, while the cooler inner layer remains smooth.

PINWHEEL On *cut glass*, a design resembling a hobstar in motion; its points angled in a clockwise or counterclockwise position.

PONTIL MARK Rough spot caused by breaking away the pontil rod.

PONTIL ROD A rod or iron used by glassworkers to hold the glass while it is being formed.

POT A one-piece container in which glass is melted, usually made of clay and able to withstand extreme heat.

PLINTH A square block forming the base for a standard. Also, a base and standard molded in one piece, used as the lower unit of a lamp.

PRESSED GLASS Glass made by placing hot glass into a mold and forcing it with a plunger to conform to the shape of the mold.

PRISM A pattern or design of deep parallel V-grooves that reflect the light.

PRUNT A blob of glass applied to the surface of a vessel, for the purpose of decorating or hiding a defect.

PUNTING The process of dishing out a circle with a cutting wheel, usually to remove the mark left by the pontil rod.

PUNTY A concave circle made by dishing out the glass with a cutting wheel.

QUILTING In *art glass*, an all-over diamond design, permanently molded into the piece as it was being blown.

RIBBON ROD A rod that has twisted flat ribbons of glass running through it.

RIGAREE A heavy thread of glass applied to the surface of a piece, giving a decorative rippled or fluted effect.

ROD A straight shaft of glass that will be reheated to form other things. Thin rods are fused together to make canes, and are also softened to supply glass for lampwork. Thick rods are formed into chandelier arms and epergne units. Reeded rods are used to form handles and claw feet on Late Blown Ware, as well as nibs for glass writing pens.

SERVITOR The first assistant to the gaffer in a group of glassworkers called a *shop*.

SHEDDING The flaking of the surface of finished glass exposed to the air, cause by minute particles of fire clay in the sand. According to C. C. P. Waterman, writing in 1875, " . . . small specks of fire clay which shed themselves very much to their annoyance throughout the melted glass."

SHELL FOOT   See *claw foot*.

SHOP   A group of workmen producing glass at the furnace, consisting of a master glass blower and his help.

SICK GLASS   Discoloration of the surface of an article.

SLOAR BOOK   The book in which an accounting was kept of the output of glass produced by each shop at the furnace.

SLOAR MAN   The glassworker who entered the output of each shop in the sloar book.

SOCKET EXTENSION   On a *candlestick*, the section between the socket and the wafer, molded in one piece with the socket.

SPIDER PONTIL   An iron unit placed on the end of the pontil rod, consisting of several finger-like rods. The fingers gave support to items that could not be held by a single rod in the center.

STAINED GLASS   A finished piece of clear glass that is colored wholly or in part by the application of a chemical dye—most commonly ruby. The article is re-fired, making the dye a permanent finish.

STICKER-UP BOY   The boy who carries hot glass on a V-shaped stick in a group of glassworkers called a *shop*.

STRAWBERRY DIAMOND   On *cut glass*, a diamond which is crosshatched. Also the name of a cut glass design that utilizes crosscut diamonds.

TAKER-IN BOY   The boy who carries the hot finished product to the leer in a group of glassworkers called a *shop*. During slow periods, he assists in the removal of glass from the cold end of the leer.

TALE   Articles sold by count rather than by weight. In the words of Deming Jarves, "Tale was derived from the mode of selling, the best glass being sold only by weight, while light articles were sold tale."

UNDERFILL   An insufficient amount of glass blown or pressed into a mold, resulting in an incomplete product. This is a characteristic, not a defect.

VESICA   On *cut glass*, a pointed oval.

WAFER   A flattened piece of hot glass, sometimes called a merese, used to join separately made units into a complete piece, such as the base and socket of a candlestick or the bowl and standard of a footed nappie.

WHIMSEY   Unusual, one-of-a-kind item made of glass by a worker in his spare time.

INVENTORY OF SANDWICH GLASS

No.	Description	Condition	Date Purchased	Amount	Date Sold	Amount

BIBLIOGRAPHY

UNPUBLISHED SOURCES

Account book of various activities of the Boston and Sandwich Glass Company, such as the company store, seagoing vessels, wages, and wood for construction and fuel. April 17, 1826, to July 1830. Ms. collection in the Tannahill Research Library, Henry Ford Museum, Edison Institute, Dearborn, Michigan.

Burbank, George E. *History of the Sandwich Glass Works.* Ms. in the Barlow collection.

Corporate records. Office of the Secretary of State, The Commonwealth of Massachusetts, Boston, Massachusetts.

Correspondence pertaining to the management of the Boston and Sandwich Glass Company and the Cape Cod Glass Company, such as glass formulas, letters, special notices and transfers. Ms. collection in the Tannahill Research Library, Henry Ford Museum, Edison Institute, Dearborn, Michigan.

Correspondence pertaining to the management of the Boston and Sandwich Glass Company, the Boston and Sandwich Glass Company II and the Cape Cod Glass Company, such as glass formulas, letters, statements, etc. Ms. collection in the Rakow Library, The Corning Museum of Glass, Corning, New York.

Correspondence to and from glass authorities and writers on the subject of glass, pertaining to the excavation of the Boston and Sandwich Glass Company site and the discussion of fragments. Ms. consisting of the Francis (Bill) Wynn papers, now in the Barlow collection.

Documentation in the form of fragments dug from factory and cutting shop sites. Private collections and the extensive Barlow collection, which includes the former Francis (Bill) Wynn collection.

Documentation of Sandwich glass items and Sandwich glassworkers, such as hand-written notebooks, letters, billheads, contracts, pictures, and oral history of Sandwich families recorded on tape by descendants. Ms. in the Barlow collection, Kaiser collection and private collections.

Documents pertaining to the genealogy of the family of Deming Jarves. Mount Auburn Cemetery, Cambridge, Massachusetts.

Documents pertaining to the Sandwich glass industry and other related industries, such as statistics from Sandwich Vital Records, information from property tax records, maps, photographs, family papers and genealogy. Ms. in the care of the Town of Sandwich Massachusetts Archives and Historical Center, Sandwich, Massachusetts.

Documents relating to the North Sandwich industrial area, such as photographs, account books and handwritten scrapbooks. Ms. in the private collection of Mrs. Edward "Ned" Nickerson and the Bourne Historical Society, Bourne, Massachusetts.

Documents relating to the Sandwich Co-operative Glass Company, such as account books, correspondence and glass formulas. Ms. in the private collection of Murray family descendants.

Glass formula book. "Sandwich Aug. 7, 1868, James D. Lloyd." Ms. collection in the Tannahill Research Library, Henry Ford Museum, Edison Institute, Dearborn, Michigan.

Lapham family documents, such as pictures and genealogy. Ms. in the private collections of Lapham family descendants.

Lutz family documents, such as pictures, handwritten biographies and genealogy. Ms. in the private collections of Lutz family descendants.

Mary Gregory documents, such as diaries, letters and pictures. Ms. in the Barlow collection, Kaiser collection, other private collections, and included in the private papers of her family.

Minutes of annual meetings, Board of Directors meetings, special meetings and stockholders meetings of the Boston and Sandwich Glass Company. Ms. collection in the Tannahill Research Library, Henry Ford Museum, Edison Institute, Dearborn, Michigan.

Minutes of meetings of the American Flint Glass Workers Union, Local No. 16. Ms. in the Sandwich Glass Museum, Sandwich Historical Society, Sandwich, Massachusetts.

Nye family documents relating to the North Sandwich industrial area and the Electrical Glass Corporation. Ms. in the Barlow-Kaiser collection.

Oral history recorded on tape. Tales of Cape Cod, Inc. collection in the Cape Cod Community College Library, Hyannis, Massachusetts.

Patents relating to the invention of new techniques in glassmaking, improved equipment for glassmaking, new designs and styles of glass, and the invention of other items relating to the glass industry. United States Department of Commerce, Patent and Trademark Office, Washington, D. C.

Population Schedule of the Census of the United States. Ms. from National Archives Microfilm Publications, National Archives and Records Service, Washington, D. C.

Property deeds and other proofs of ownership, such as surveys, mortagage deeds, and last will and testaments. Ms. in the Barnstable County Registry of Deeds and Barnstable County Registry of Probate, Barnstable, Massachusetts.

Sloar book, a weekly accounting of glass produced at the Sandwich Glass Manufactory and the Boston and Sandwich Glass Company, and the workers who produced it. July 9, 1825, to March 29, 1828. Ms. collection in the Tannahill Research Library, Henry Ford Museum, Edison Institute, Dearborn, Michigan.

Spurr family documents, such as pictures, handwritten autobiographies, glass formulas and genealogy. Ms. in the private collections of Spurr family descendants.

Vodon family documents, such as pictures and genealogy. Ms. in the private collection of Vodon family descendants.

Waterman, Charles Cotesworth Pinckney. Notes on the Boston and Sandwich Glass Company, dated November 1876, and deposited in the Sandwich Centennial Box. Ms. in the care of the Town of Sandwich Massachusetts Archives and Historical Center, Sandwich, Massachusetts.

PRINTED SOURCES

Amic, Yolande. *L'Opaline Francaise au XIXe Siecle*. Paris, France: Library Gründ, 1952.

Anthony, T. Robert. *19th Century Fairy Lamps*. Manchester, Vermont: Forward's Color Productions, Inc., 1969.

Avila, George C. *The Pairpoint Glass Story*. New Bedford, Massachusetts: Reynolds-DeWalt Printing, Inc., 1968.

Barbour, Harriot Buxton. *Sandwich The Town That Glass Built*. Boston, Massachusetts: Houghton Mifflin Company, 1948.

Barret, Richard Carter. *A Collectors Handbook of American Art Glass*. Manchester, Vermont: Forward's Color Productions, Inc., 1971.

_____. *A Collectors Handbook of Blown and Pressed American Glass*. Manchester, Vermont: Forward's Color Productions, Inc., 1971.

_____. *Popular American Ruby-Stained Pattern Glass*. Manchester, Vermont: Forward's Color Productions, Inc., 1968.

Belknap, E. McCamly. *Milk Glass*. New York, New York: Crown Publishers, Inc., 1949.

Bishop, Barbara. "Deming Jarves and His Glass Factories," *The Glass Club Bulletin*, Spring 1983, pp. 3-5.

Bishop, Barbara and Martha Hassell. *Your Obd^t. Servt., Deming Jarves*. Sandwich, Massachusetts: The Sand-

wich Historical Society, 1984.

Brown, Clark W. *Salt Dishes*. Leon, Iowa: Mid-America Book Company, reprinted in 1968.

_____. *A Supplement to Salt Dishes*. Leon, Iowa: Prairie Winds Press, reprinted in 1970.

Burbank, George E. *A Bit of Sandwich History*. Sandwich, Massachusetts: 1939.

Burgess, Bangs. *History of Sandwich Glass*. Yarmouth, Massachusetts: The Register Press, 1925.

Butterfield, Oliver. "Bewitching Witchballs," *Yankee*, July 1978, pp. 97, 172-175.

Cataldo, Louis and Dorothy Worrell. *Pictorial Tales of Cape Cod*. (Vol. I) Hyannis, Massachusetts: Tales of Cape Cod, Inc., 1956.

Cataldo, Louis and Dorothy Worrell. *Pictorial Tales of Cape Cod*. (Vol. II) Hyannis, Massachusetts: Tales of Cape Cod, Inc., 1961.

Childs, David B. "If It's Threaded . . . ," *Yankee*, June 1960, pp. 86-89.

Chipman, Frank W. *The Romance of Old Sandwich Glass*. Sandwich, Massachusetts: Sandwich Publishing Company Inc., 1932.

Cloak, Evelyn Campbell. *Glass Paperweights of the Bergstrom Art Center*. New York, New York: Crown Publishers, Inc., 1969.

Covill, William E., Jr. *Ink Bottles and Inkwells*. Taunton, Massachusetts: William S. Sullwold Publishing, 1971.

Culver, Willard R. "From Sand to Seer and Servant of Man," *The National Geographic Magazine*, January 1943, pp. 17-24, 41-48.

Deyo, Simeon L. *History of Barnstable County, Massachusetts*. New York, New York: H. W. Blake & Co., 1890.

DiBartolomeo, Robert E. *American Glass from the Pages of Antiques; Pressed and Cut*. (Vol. II) Princeton, New Jersey: The Pyne Press, 1974.

Dooley, William Germain. *Old Sandwich Glass*. Pasadena, California: Esto Publishing Company, n.d.

_____. "Recollections of Sandwich Glass by a Veteran Who Worked on It," *Hobbies*, June 1951, p. 96.

Drepperd, Carl W. *The ABC's of Old Glass*. Garden City, New York: Doubleday & Company, Inc., 1949.

Fauster, Carl U. *Libbey Glass Since 1818*. Toledo, Ohio: Len Beach Press, 1979.

Freeman, Frederick. *History of Cape Cod: Annals of the Thirteen Towns of Barnstable County*. Boston, Massachusetts: George C. Rand & Avery, 1862.

Freeman, Dr. Larry. *New Light on Old Lamps*. Watkins Glen, New York: American Life Foundation, reprinted in 1984.

Gaines, Edith. "Woman's Day Dictionary of American Glass," *Woman's Day*, August 1961, pp. 19-34.

_____. "Woman's Day Dictionary of Sandwich Glass," *Woman's Day*, August 1963, pp. 21-32.

_____. "Woman's Day Dictionary of Victorian Glass," *Woman's Day*, August 1964, pp. 23-34.

Gores, Stan. *1876 Centennial Collectibles and Price Guide*. Fond du Lac, Wisconsin: The Haber Printing Co., 1974.

Grover, Ray and Lee Grover. *Art Glass Nouveau*. Rutland, Vermont: Charles E. Tuttle Company, Inc., 1967.

Grover, Ray and Lee Grover. *Carved & Decorated European Art Glass*. Rutland, Vermont: Charles E. Tuttle Company, Inc., 1970.

Grow, Lawrence. *The Warner Collector's Guide to Pressed Glass*. New York, New York: Warner Books, Inc., 1982.

Hammond, Dorothy. *Confusing Collectibles*. Des Moines, Iowa: Wallace-Homestead Book Company, 1969.

_____. *More Confusing Collectibles*. Wichita, Kansas: C. B. P. Publishing Company, 1972.

Harris, Amanda B. "Down in Sandwich Town," *Wide Awake* 1, 1887, pp. 19-27.

Harris, John. *The Great Boston Fire, 1872*. Boston, Massachusetts: Boston Globe, 1972.

Hartung, Marion T. and Ione E. Hinshaw. *Patterns and Pinafores*. Des Moines, Iowa: Wallace-Homestead Book Company, 1971.

Haynes, E. Barrington. *Glass Through the Ages*. Baltimore, Maryland: Penguin Books, 1969.

Hayward, Arthur H. *Colonial and Early American Lighting*. New York, New York: Dover Publications, Inc., reprinted in 1962.

Heacock, William. *Encyclopedia of Victorian Colored Pattern Glass; Book 1 Toothpick Holders from A to Z*. Jonesville, Michigan: Antique Publications, 1974.

_____. *Encyclopedia of Victorian Colored Pattern Glass; Book 2 Opalescent Glass from A to Z*. Jonesville, Michigan: Antique Publications, 1975.

_____. *Encyclopedia of Victorian Colored Pattern Glass; Book 3 Syrups, Sugar Shakers & Cruets from A to Z*. Jonesville, Michigan: Antique Publications, 1976.

_____. *Encyclopedia of Victorian Colored Pattern Glass; Book 4 Custard Glass from A to Z*. Marietta, Ohio: Antique Publications, 1976.

_____. *Encyclopedia of Victorian Colored Pattern Glass; Book 5 U. S. Glass from A to Z*. Marietta, Ohio: Antique Publications, 1978.

_____. *Encyclopedia of Victorian Colored Pattern Glass; Book 6 Oil Cruets from A to Z*. Marietta, Ohio: Antique Publications, 1981.

_____. *1000 Toothpick Holders; A Collector's Guide*. Marietta, Ohio: Antique Publications, 1977.

Heacock, William and Patricia Johnson. *5000 Open Salts; A Collector's Guide*. Marietta, Ohio: Richardson Printing Corporation, 1982.

Heckler, Norman. *American Bottles in the Charles B. Gardner Collection*. Bolton, Massachusetts: Robert W. Skinner, Inc., 1975.

Hildebrand, J. R. "Glass Goes To Town," *The National Geographic Magazine*, January 1943, pp. 1-16, 25-40.

Hollister, Paul, Jr. *The Encyclopedia of Glass Paperweights*. New York, New York: Clarkson N. Potter, Inc., 1969.

Ingold, Gérard. *The Art of the Paperweight; Saint Louis*. Santa Cruz, California: Paperweight Press, 1981.

Innes, Lowell. *Pittsburgh Glass 1797-1891*. Boston, Massachusetts: Houghton Mifflin Company, 1976.

Irwin, Frederick T. *The Story of Sandwich Glass*. Manchester, New Hampshire: Granite State Press, 1926.

Jarves, Deming. *Reminiscences of Glass-making*. Great Neck, New York: Beatrice C. Weinstock, reprinted in 1968.

Kamm, Minnie W. and Serry Wood. *The Kamm-Wood Encyclopedia of Pattern Glass*. (II vols.) Watkins Glen, New York: Century House, 1961.

Keene, Betsey D. *History of Bourne 1622-1937*. Yarmouthport, Massachusetts: Charles W. Swift, 1937.

Knittle, Rhea Mansfield. *Early American Glass*. New York, New York: The Century Co., 1927.

Lane, Lyman and Sally Lane, and Joan Pappas. *A Rare Collection of Keene & Stoddard Glass*. Manchester, Vermont: Forward's Color Productions, Inc., 1970.

Lanmon, Dwight P. "Russian Paperweights and Letter Seals?" *The Magazine Antiques*, October 1984, pp. 900-903.

_____. "Unmasking an American Glass Fraud," *The Magazine Antiques*, January 1983, pp. 226-236.

Lechler, Doris Anderson. *Children's Glass Dishes, China, and Furniture*. Paducah, Kentucky: Collector Books, 1983.

Lechler, Doris and Virginia O'Neill. *Children's Glass Dishes*. Nashville, Tennessee, 1976.

Lee, Ruth Webb. *Antique Fakes & Reproductions*. Wellesley Hills, Massachusetts: Lee Publications, 1966.

_____. *Early American Pressed Glass*. Wellesley Hills, Massachusetts: Lee Publications, 1960.

_____. *Nineteenth-Century Art Glass*. New York, New York: M. Barrows & Company, Inc., 1952.

_____. *Sandwich Glass*. Wellesley Hills, Massachusetts: Lee Publications, 1939.

_____. *Victorian Glass*. Wellesley Hills, Massachusetts: Lee Publications, 1944.

Lee, Ruth Webb and James H. Rose. *American Glass Cup Plates*. Wellesley Hills, Massachusetts: Lee Publications, 1948.

Lindsey, Bessie M. *American Historical Glass*. Rutland, Vermont: Charles E. Tuttle Co., 1967.

Lovell, Russell A., Jr. *The Cape Cod Story of Thornton W. Burgess*. Taunton, Massachusetts: Thornton W. Burgess Society, Inc., and William S. Sullwold Publishing, 1974.

_____. *Sandwich; A Cape Cod Town*. Sandwich, Massachusetts: Town of Sandwich Massachusetts Archives and Historical Center, 1984.

Mackay, James. *Glass Paperweights*. New York, New York: The Viking Press, Inc., 1973.

Manheim, Frank J. *A Garland of Weights*. New York, New York: Farrar, Straus and Giroux, 1967.

Manley, C. C. *British Glass*. Des Moines, Iowa: Wallace-Homestead Book Co., 1968.

Manley, Cyril. *Decorative Victorian Glass*. New York, New York: Van Nostrand Reinhold Company, 1981.

Mannoni, Edith. *Opalines*. Paris, France: Éditions Ch. Massin, n.d.

McKearin, George S. and Helen McKearin. *American Glass*. New York, New York: Crown Publishers, Inc., 1941.

McKearin, Helen and George S. McKearin. *Two Hundred Years of American Blown Glass*. New York, New York: Bonanza Books, 1949.

McKearin, Helen and Kenneth M. Wilson. *American Bottles & Flasks and Their Ancestry*. New York, New York: Crown Publishers, Inc., 1978.

Measell, James. *Greentown Glass; The Indiana Tumbler and Goblet Company.* Grand Rapids, Michigan: The Grand Rapids Public Museum with the Grand Rapids Museum Association, 1979.

Metz, Alice Hulett. *Early American Pattern Glass.* Columbus, Ohio: Spencer-Walker Press, 1965.

_____. *Much More Early American Pattern Glass.* Columbus, Ohio: Spencer-Walker Press, 1970.

Millard, S. T. *Goblets II.* Holton, Kansas: Gossip Printers and Publishers, 1940.

Miller, Robert W. *Mary Gregory and Her Glass.* Des Moines, Iowa: Wallace-Homestead Book Co., 1972.

Moore, N. Hudson. *Old Glass.* New York, New York: Tudor Publishing Co., 1924.

Mulch, Dwight. "John D. Larkin and Company: From Factory to Family," *The Antique Trader Weekly,* June 24, 1984, pp. 92-94.

Neal, L. W. and D. B. Neal. *Pressed Glass Salt Dishes of the Lacy Period 1825-1850.* Philadelphia, Pennsylvania: L. W. and D. B. Neal, 1962.

Pearson, J. Michael and Dorothy T. Pearson. *American Cut Glass Collections.* Miami, Florida: The Franklin Press, Inc., 1969.

Pearson, J. Michael and Dorothy T. Pearson. *American Cut Glass for the Discriminating Collector.* Miami, Florida: The Franklin Press, Inc., 1965.

Pepper, Adeline. *The Glass Gaffers of New Jersey.* New York, New York: Charles Scribner's Sons, 1971.

Peterson, Arthur G. *Glass Patents and Patterns.* Sanford, Florida: Celery City Printing Co., 1973.

_____. *Glass Salt Shakers: 1,000 Patterns.* Des Moines, Iowa: Wallace-Homestead Book Co., 1960.

Raycraft, Don and Carol Raycraft. *Early American Lighting.* Des Moines, Iowa: Wallace-Homestead Book Co., n.d.

Revi, Albert Christian. *American Art Nouveau Glass.* Exton, Pennsylvania: Schiffer Publishing, Ltd., 1981.

_____. *American Cut and Engraved Glass.* Nashville, Tennessee: Thomas Nelson Inc., 1972.

_____. *American Pressed Glass and Figure Bottles.* Nashville, Tennessee: Thomas Nelson Inc., 1972.

_____. *Nineteenth Century Glass.* Exton, Pennsylvania: Schiffer Publishing, Ltd., 1967.

Righter, Miriam. *Iowa City Glass.* Des Moines, Iowa: Wallace-Homestead Book Co., 1966.

Robertson, Frank E. "New Evidence from Sandwich Glass Fragments," *The Magazine Antiques,* October 1982, pp. 818-823.

Robertson, R. A. *Chats on Old Glass.* New York, New York: Dover Publications, Inc., 1969. Revised and enlarged by Kenneth M. Wilson.

Rose, James H. *The Story of American Pressed Glass of the Lacy Period 1825-1850.* Corning, New York: The Corning Museum of Glass, 1954.

Rushlight Club. *Early Lighting; A Pictorial Guide.* Talcottville, Connecticut: 1972.

Sandwich Glass Museum. *The Sandwich Glass Museum Collection.* Sandwich, Massachusetts: Sandwich Glass Museum, 1969.

Sauzay, A. *Wonders of Art and Archaeology; Wonders of Glass Making.* New York, New York: Charles Scribner's Sons, 1885.

Schwartz, Marvin D. *American Glass from the Pages of Antiques; Blown and Moulded.* (Vol. I) Princeton, New Jersey: The Pyne Press, 1974.

Smith, Allan B. and Helen B. Smith. *One Thousand Individual Open Salts Illustrated.* Litchfield, Maine: The Country House, 1972.

Smith, Allan B. and Helen B. Smith. *650 More Individual Open Salts Illustrated.* Litchfield, Maine: The Country House, 1973.

Smith, Allan B. and Helen B. Smith. *The Third Book of Individual Open Salts Illustrated.* Litchfield, Maine: The Country House, 1976.

Smith, Allan B. and Helen B. Smith. *Individual Open Salts Illustrated.* Litchfield, Maine: The Country House, n.d.

Smith, Allan B. and Helen B. Smith. *Individual Open Salts Illustrated; 1977 Annual.* Litchfield, Maine: The Country House, 1977.

Smith, Frank R. and Ruth E. Smith. *Miniature Lamps.* New York, New York: Thomas Nelson Inc., 1968.

Spillman, Jane Shadel. *American and European Pressed Glass in The Corning Museum of Glass.* Corning, New York: The Corning Museum of Glass, 1981.

_____. *Glass Bottles, Lamps & Other Objects.* New York, New York: Alfred A. Knopf, Inc., 1983.

_____. *Glass Tableware, Bowls & Vases.* New York, New York: Alfred A. Knopf, Inc., 1982.

_____. "Pressed-Glass Designs in the United States and Europe," *The Magazine Antiques,* July 1983, pp. 130-139.

Stanley, Mary Louise. *A Century of Glass Toys.* Manchester, Vermont: Forward's Color Productions, Inc., n.d.

Stetson, Nelson M. *Booklet No. 6; Stetson Kindred of America.* Campbello, Massachusetts: 1923.

Stow, Charles Messer. *The Deming Jarves Book of Designs.* Yarmouth, Massachusetts: The Register Press, 1925.

Swan, Frank H. *Portland Glass.* Des Moines, Iowa: Wallace-Homestead Book Company, 1949. Revised and enlarged by Marion Dana.

_____. *Portland Glass Company.* Providence, Rhode Island: The Roger Williams Press, 1939.

Taylor, Katrina V. H. "Russian Glass in the Hillwood Museum." *The Magazine Antiques,* July 1983, pp. 140-145.

Teleki, Gloria Roth. *The Baskets of Rural America.* New York, New York: E. P. Dutton & Co., Inc., 1975.

The Toledo Museum of Art. *Art in Glass.* Toledo, Ohio: The Toledo Museum of Art, 1969.

_____. *The New England Glass Company 1818-1888.* Toledo, Ohio: The Toledo Museum of Art, 1963.

Thuro, Catherine M. V. *Oil Lamps; The Kerosene Era in North America.* Des Moines, Iowa: Wallace-Homestead Book Co., 1976.

_____. *Oil Lamps II; Glass Kerosene Lamps.* Paducah, Kentucky and Des Moines, Iowa: Collector Books and Wallace-Homestead Book Co., 1983.

Thwing, Leroy. *Flickering Flames.* Rutland, Vermont: Charles E. Tuttle Company, 1974.

Towne, Sumner. "Mike Grady's Last Pot," *Yankee,* March 1968, pp. 84, 85, 136-139.

VanRensselaer, Stephen. *Early American Bottles & Flasks.*

Stratford, Connecticut: J. Edmund Edwards, 1971.

Vuilleumier, Marion. *Cape Cod; a Pictorial History.* Norfolk, Virginia, 1982.

Walsh, Lavinia. "The Romance of Sandwich Glass," *The Cape Cod Magazine*, July 1926, pp. 9, 26.

_____. "Old Boston and Sandwich Glassworks . . . .," *Ceramic Age*, December 1950, pp. 16, 17, 34.

Watkins, Lura Woodside. *American Glass and Glassmaking.* New York, New York: Chanticleer Press, 1950.

_____. *Cambridge Glass 1818 to 1888.* New York, New York: Bramhall House, 1930.

Webber, Norman W. *Collecting Glass.* New York, New York: Arco Publishing Company, Inc., 1973.

Webster, Noah. *An American Dictionary of the English Language.* Springfield, Massachusetts: George and Charles Merriam, 1847. Revised.

_____. *An American Dictionary of the English Language.* Springfield, Massachusetts: George and Charles Merriam, 1859. Revised and enlarged by Chauncey A. Goodrich.

_____. *An American Dictionary of the English Language.* Springfield, Massachusetts: G. & C. Merriam, 1872. Revised and enlarged by Chauncey A. Goodrich and Noah Porter.

Wetz, Jon and Jacqueline Wetz. *The Co-operative Glass Company Sandwich, Massachusetts: 1888*-1891. Sandwich, Massachusetts: Barn Lantern Publishing, 1976.

Williams, Lenore Wheeler. *Sandwich Glass.* Bridgeport, Connecticut: The Park City Eng. Co., 1922.

Wilson, Kenneth M. *New England Glass & Glassmaking.* New York, New York: Thomas Y. Crowell Company, 1972.

CATALOGS

A. L. Blackmer Co. Rich Cut Glass 1906-1907. Shreveport, Louisiana: The American Cut Glass Association, reprinted in 1982.

Amberina; 1884 New England Glass Works; 1917 Libbey Glass Company. Toledo, Ohio: Antique & Historical Glass Foundation, reprinted in 1970.

Averbeck Rich Cut Glass Catalog No. 104, The. Berkeley, California: Cembura & Avery Publishers, reprinted in 1973.

Boston & Sandwich Glass Co., Boston. Wellesley Hills, Massachusetts: Lee Publications, reprinted in 1968.

Boston & Sandwich Glass Co. Price List. Collection of the Sandwich Glass Museum, Sandwich Historical Society, Sandwich, Massachusetts, n.d.

Catalog of 700 Packages Flint Glass Ware Manufactured by the Cape Cod Glass Works, to be Sold at the New England Trade Sale, Wednesday, July 14, 1859 at 9½ O'clock. Collection of The Corning Museum of Glass Library, Corning, New York, 1859.

C. Dorflinger & Sons Cut Glass Catalog. Silver Spring, Maryland: Christian Dorflinger Glass Study Group, reprinted in 1981.

Collector's Paperweights; Price Guide and Catalog. Santa Cruz, California: Paperweight Press, 1983.

Cut Glass Produced by the Laurel Cut Glass Company. Shreveport, Louisiana: The American Cut Glass Associ-

ation, reprinted, n.d.

Egginton's Celebrated Cut Glass. Shreveport, Louisiana: The American Cut Glass Association, reprinted in 1982.

Empire Cut Glass Company, The. Shreveport, Louisiana: American Cut Glass Association, reprinted in 1980.

F. X. Parsche & Son Co. Shreveport, Louisiana: American Cut Glass Association, reprinted in 1981.

Glassware Catalogue No. 25 Gillinder & Sons, Inc. Spring City, Tennessee: Hillcrest Books, reprinted in 1974.

Higgins and Seiter Fine China and Cut Glass Catalog No. 13. New York, New York: Higgins and Seiter, n.d.

Illustrated Catalog of American Hardware of the Russell and Erwin Manufacturing Company 1865. Association for Preservation Technology, reprinted in 1980.

J. D. Bergen Co., The; Manufacturers of Rich Cut Glassware 1904-1905. Berkeley, California: Cembura & Avery Publishers, reprinted in 1973.

Lackawanna Cut Glass Co. Shreveport, Louisiana: The American Cut Glass Association, reprinted, n.d.

Launay Hautin & Cie. Collection de dessins representant . . . Collection of The Corning Museum of Glass Library, Corning, New York, n.d.

Launay Hautin & Cie. Des Fabriques de Baccarat, St. Louis, Choisey et Bercy. Collection of The Corning Museum of Glass Library, Corning, New York, n.d.

Launay Hautin & Cie. Repertoire des Articles compris dans la Collection . . . Collection of The Corning Museum of Glass Library, Corning, New York, 1844.

Launay Hautin & Cie. Usages principaux pour services de table . . . Collection of The Corning Museum of Glass Library, Corning, New York, n.d.

Libbey Glass Co., The; Cut Glass June 1st, 1896. Toledo, Ohio: Antique & Historical Glass Foundation, reprinted in 1968.

List of Glass Ware Manufactured by Cape Cod Glass Company. Collection of the Sandwich Glass Museum, Sandwich Historical Society, Sandwich, Massachusetts, n.d.

M'Kee Victorial Glass; Five Complete Glass Catalogs from 1859/60 to 1871. New York, New York: Dover Publications, Inc., reprinted in 1981.

Monroe Cut Glass. Shreveport, Louisiana: American Cut Glass Association, reprinted, n.d.

Morey, Churchill & Morey Pocket Guide to 1880 Table Settings. Watkins Glen, New York: Century House, reprinted, n.d.

Mt. Washington Glass Co. Clinton, Maryland: Leonard E. Padgett, reprinted in 1976.

Mt. Washington Glass Company (cut glassware). Collection of The Corning Museum of Glass Library, Corning, New York, n.d.

Mt. Washington Glass Company; Crystal Gas Fixtures. Collection of The Corning Museum of Glass Library, Corning, New York, n.d.

Mt. Washington Glass Works (glass prisms and beads). Collection of The Corning Museum of Glass Library, Corning, New York, n.d.

Mt. Washington Glass Works Price List. Collection of The Corning Museum of Glass Library, Corning, New York, n.d.

New England Glass Company. Collection of The Corning Museum of Glass Library, Corning, New York, n.d.

New England Glass Company (list of glassware). Collection of The Corning Museum of Glass Library, Corning, New York, n.d.

Picture Book of Authentic Mid-Victorian Gas Lighting Fixtures; A Reprint of the Historic Mitchell, Vance & Co. Catalog, ca. 1876, with Over 1000 Illustrations. Mineola, New York: Dover Publications, Inc., reprinted in 1984.

Public Auction Richard A. Bourne Company, Inc. Boston, Massachusetts: The Nimrod Press, Inc., 1970–1985.

Quaker City Cut Glass Co. Shreveport, Louisiana: American Cut Glass Association, n.d.

Rich Cut Glass Pitkin & Brooks. Berkeley, California: Cembura & Avery Publishers, reprinted in 1973.

Sandwich Glass Patterns. West Englewood, New Jersey: Bernadine Forgett, n.d.

Taylor Bros. & Company, Inc., Manufacturers of Cut Glass. Shreveport, Louisiana: American Cut Glass Association, n.d.

BUSINESS DIRECTORIES

Boston City Directories. 1789–1891.

Resident and Business Directory of Bourne, Falmouth and Sandwich, Massachusetts. Hopkinton, Massachusetts: A. E. Foss & Co., 1900

NEWSPAPERS AND TRADE PAPERS

Academy Breezes. 1884–1886.

Acorn, The. Sandwich, Massachusetts: The Sandwich Historical Society, 1967–1985.

American Collector. New York, New York: Educational Publishing Corporation, 1933–1946.

Barnstable Patriot. 1830–1869.

Barnstable Patriot, The. 1869–1905, 1912–1916, 1918–1923.

Bourne Pioneer, The. 1906–1907.

Brockton Searchlight, The. 1909.

Cape Cod Advocate, and Nautical Intelligencer. 1851–1864.

Cape Cod Gazette. 1870–1872.

Casino Bulletin. 1884–1885.

Chronicle of the Early American Industries Association, The. Flushing, New York: Leon S. Case, January 1938.

Crockery & Glass Journal. New York, New York: George Whittemore & Company, 1885–1890.

Crockery Journal. New York, New York: George Whittemore & Company, 1874–1884.

Glass Club Bulletin, The. The National Early American Glass Club, 1938–1985.

Hyannis Patriot, The. 1908–1909, 1916–1918, 1923–1925.

Independent, The. 1895–1908.

Sandwich Collector, The. East Sandwich, Massachusetts: McCue Publications, 1984–1985.

Sandwich Independent. 1920–1921.

Sandwich Independent, The. 1908–1909.

Sandwich Mechanic and Family Visitor. 1851.

Sandwich Observer. 1846–1851.

Sandwich Observer, The. 1884–1895, 1910–1911.

Sandwich Review, The. 1889–1890.

Seaside Press, The. 1873–1880.

Village Broadsider, The. 1978–1985.

Weekly Review, The. 1881–1882.

Yarmouth Register and Barnstable County Advertiser. 1836–1839.

Yarmouth Register and Barnstable County Weekly Advertiser. 1839–1846.

Yarmouth Register. 1849–1906.

BARLOW-KAISER
SANDWICH GLASS
PRICE GUIDE
for pieces in perfect condition

SECOND EDITION

to be used with Volumes 3 and 4 of
THE GLASS INDUSTRY IN SANDWICH
and
A GUIDE TO SANDWICH GLASS

INTRODUCTION TO PRICE GUIDE

It is most important to determine the condition of a glass item before you purchase it. We are often so fascinated by a good "find" that we miss its obvious condition. The prices in this guide are for items that are in perfect, or *mint*, condition. *Mint condition* is an article of glass that is pristine. It has no defects. If there is roughage only in places where there are mold marks, it is still considered to be mint, because if the item was good enough to pass inspection at the time of production, it is good enough to be called mint today. Shear marks (often called "straw marks"), caused by cutting through a glob of glass while it was hot, do not detract from value. They are a fact of construction procedure. Manufacturing errors, such as annealing marks, bent or twisted pieces, off-center pieces, underfilled or overfilled molds, and overheating, add character to a piece of glass. However, the mint condition status of the glass is not affected. Rapid reductions in pricing are caused by damage after the time of manufacture in the following order, using the 100% value of a mint item as a base.

CONDITION	MAXIMUM VALUE OF MINT
CHIPPED Damage serious enough to penetrate into the body of an article, but small or shallow enough so that it cannot be glued back or replaced.	80%
BRUISED When an article has been struck with enough force to send cracks in several directions, penetrating the surface at the center.	60%
CRACKED When the glass is split through one or more layers, caused by a blow, a change in temperature, or stress in the glass at the time of manufacture. This is the first stage of deterioration, leading to eventual destruction. Value is seriously affected	50%
BROKEN An article is broken when it is in two pieces, even though one of the pieces may only be the tip of a scallop, or the corner of a base, or the peg of a lamp font. If one piece must be glued back in order to make the article whole, the article is broken and its value must be reduced accordingly.	25%

An unusually rare article, even though broken, must be considered for purchase regardless of price, if the serious collector is to have an example of that article.

VASES AND FLOWER CONTAINERS

A single vase is worth less than 50% of a matching pair. When you are pricing vases, make sure you have a matching pair and not two single vases. Unlike candlesticks and lamps, vases that were pressed were made in single colors only.

Photo No.	Clear	Clambroth (Alabaster)	Opaque White	Canary	Amber	Blue	Amethyst	Green	Unusual Color
3001 a	45 ea.			160 ea.		180 ea.	180 ea.		
b				12 ea.		12 ea.	12 ea.	15 ea.	12 ea. ruby
3002				400 pr.			550 pr.		
3003		200 ea. fiery opalescent			200 ea.	160 ea.	160 ea.		250 ea. lime green
3004		200 ea. fiery opalescent			200 ea.	160 ea.	160 ea.		250 ea. lime green
3005	15 ea.			60 ea.		60 ea.	75 ea.		
3006	20 ea.								
3007	115 ea.								
3008	1200 pr.								
3009	85 ea.								
3010	95 ea.								
3011	95 ea.								
3012	115 ea.								
3013	100 ea.								
3014	60 ea.	110 ea.	110 ea.	150 ea.		150 ea.	175 ea.	175 ea.	200 ea.
3015	135 pr.	300 pr.	300 pr.	450 pr.		450 pr.	500 pr.	500 pr.	600 pr.
3016	18 ea.					75 ea.	75 ea.	85 ea.	
3017	400 pr.			1200 pr.		1500 pr.	1800 pr.	2000 pr.	
3018	200 ea.			500 ea.		875 ea.	900 ea.	1000 ea.	
3019	600 pr.					2200 pr.		2400 pr.	
3020							2400 pr.		
3021	65 ea.			450 ea.	1000 ea.	875 ea.	650 ea.	1000 ea.	1200 + ea.
3022	65 ea.			450 ea.	1000 ea.	875 ea.	650 ea.	1000 ea.	1200 + ea.
3023	65 ea.			450 ea.	1000 ea.	875 ea.	650 ea.	1000 ea.	1200 + ea.
3024	85 ea.								
3025				875 ea.		1000 ea.			
3026				950 pr.	1000 pr.	1000 pr.	1000 pr.	1200 pr.	
3027		750 ea.		900 ea.			1000 ea.		
3028						875 ea.	1000 ea.		
3029				550 ea.		850 ea.		950 ea.	
3030						2400 pr.			
3031				550 ea.					
3032				875 ea.		1000 ea.			
3033	240 pr.	800 pr.		950 pr.		1400 pr.	1400 pr.	1800 pr.	
3034				1000 pr.		1450 pr.	1450 pr.	1850 pr.	
3035				450 ea.			750 ea.		
3036				450 ea.			750 ea.		
3037 a				550 ea.			750 ea.		
b							875 ea.		
3038		350 ea.		550 ea.					
3039				1800 pr.		2500 pr.		2600 pr.	
3040				850 ea.		1100 ea.		1200 ea.	
3041		700 ea. fiery opalescent	700 ea.	750 ea.				950 ea.	

Photo No.	Clear	Clambroth (Alabaster)	Opaque White	Canary	Amber	Blue	Amethyst	Green	Unusual Color
3042 a	90 ea.			400 ea.		750 ea.	750 ea.	825 ea.	
b	100 ea.			425 ea.		775 ea.	775 ea.	850 ea.	
3043 a						450 pr.			
b						225 ea.		350 ea.	
3044 a						450 pr.			
b		225 ea. with fitting	300 ea. with fitting			250 ea. with fitting	350 ea. with fitting	350 ea. with fitting	
3045		75 ea.							
3046 a						225 ea. blue and white		225 ea. green and white	
b						275 ea. blue and white		275 ea. green and white	
3047						225 ea. blue and white		225 ea. green and white	
3048 a		160 ea.				185 ea.	225 ea.		
b				200 ea.		225 ea.			

Photo No.		
3049	600 ea.	pink to white to clear Overlay, gilded
3050	150 ea.	clear
	300 ea.	opal, decorated
3051	225 ea.	
3052	200 ea.	
3053	200 ea.	
3054	600 the set	
3055	40 ea.	
3056	40 ea.	
3057	40 ea.	
3058	60 ea.	
3059	100 ea.	
3060	125 pr.	
3061	50 ea.	
3062	60 ea.	
3063	60 ea.	
3064	60 ea.	
3065	40 ea.	
3066	—	
3067	—	
3068	—	
3069	22 ea.	
3070	28 ea.	
3071	50 ea.	
3072	50 ea.	
3073	85 ea.	
3074	85 ea.	
3075	95 ea.	
3076	140 ea.	undecorated
3077	250 ea.	decorated, blue ground
	250 ea.	decorated, brown ground
	300 ea.	decorated, lilac ground
	450 ea.	decorated, colored flowers, white ground

Photo No.		
3078 a	65 ea.	
b	55 ea.	
c	45 ea.	
3079	125 ea.	
3080	95 ea.	
3081	—	
3082	225 ea.	
3083	400 ea.	
3084	600 ea.	
3085	—	
3086	—	
3087	600 ea.	
3088 a	250	stand only
b	600 ea.	
c	600 ea.	
3089 a	40 ea.	
b	28 ea.	
c	20 ea.	
3090	85 ea.	
3091	100 ea.	
3092	30 ea.	
3093	35 ea.	
3094	30 ea.	
3095	35 ea.	
3096	50 ea.	
3097	15 ea.	
3098	65 ea.	
3099	85 ea.	fiery opalescent
3100	115 ea.	fiery opalescent

COLOGNES

Cologne bottles used on dressing tables have glass stoppers. Half the value of a cologne is in its stopper.

Photo No.	Clear	Clambroth (Alabaster)	Opaque White	Canary	Amber	Blue	Amethyst	Green
3101	110 ea.	350 ea.		350 ea.		1400 ea.		2800 ea.
3102	110 ea.	350 ea.		350 ea.		1400 ea.		2800 ea.
3103	110 ea.			350 ea.				
3104				400 ea.		950 ea.		
3105	90 ea.			275 ea.				
3106	115 ea.		400 ea.	500 ea.				
3107					450 ea.	450 ea.		500 ea.
3108	190 pr.	450 pr. fiery opalescent			450 pr.			600 pr.
3109	75 ea.	175 ea. fiery opalescent			175 ea.			250 ea.
3110				250 ea.	250 ea.	275 ea.		300 ea.
3111	80 ea.					160 ea.		
3112				175 ea.	175 ea.	225 ea.	250 ea.	
3113				275 ea.		400 ea.		500 ea.
3114								500 ea.
3115					500 ea.			

Photo No.	Clear	Clambroth (Alabaster)	Opaque White	Canary	Amber	Blue	Amethyst	Green
3116			300 ea.					
3117				200 ea.		225 ea.		
3118 a						250 ea.	275 ea.	350 ea.
b	50 ea.			200 ea.				
3119						250 ea.		350 ea.
3120				225 ea.				350 ea.
3121 a						450 ea.		
b		45 ea.				65 ea.		
c		225 ea. with fitting	300 ea. with fitting			250 ea. with fitting	350 ea. with fitting	350 ea. with fitting
3122								160 ea. green and white
3123						185 ea. blue and white		185 ea. green and white
3124								350 ea.
3125		225 ea.				300 ea.		350 ea.
3126								850 ea.

Photo No.		
3127	450 ea.	
3128	—	
3129	150 ea.	
3130	160 ea.	with stopper
3131	115 ea.	
3132	135 ea.	
3133	150 ea.	
3134	110 ea.	
3135	250 ea.	blue to clear Overlay
3136	250 ea.	blue to clear Overlay
	300 ea.	ruby to clear Overlay
3137	325 ea.	blue to clear Overlay
3138	250 ea.	blue to clear Overlay
3139	300 ea.	blue to clear Overlay
	350 ea.	ruby to clear Overlay
3140	400 ea.	blue to clear Overlay
	400 ea.	ruby to clear Overlay
	600 ea.	green to clear Overlay
3141	400 ea.	blue to clear Overlay
3142	400 ea.	blue to clear Overlay
	450 ea.	ruby to clear Overlay
3143	875 ea.	ruby to clear Overlay
3144	—	
3145	575 ea.	ruby to clear Overlay
3146	650 ea.	amethyst to clear Overlay
3147	575 ea.	ruby to clear Overlay
3148	600 ea.	ruby to clear Overlay
3149	450 ea.	ruby to clear Overlay, with correct stopper
3150	500 ea.	ruby to clear Overlay
3151 a	60 ea.	ruby to clear Overlay
b	60 ea.	blue to clear Overlay

Photo No.		
3152	600 pr.	blue to clear Overlay
	750 pr.	ruby to clear Overlay
	875 pr.	green to clear Overlay
3153	110 ea.	clear
3154	300 ea.	blue to clear Overlay
	350 ea.	ruby to clear Overlay
	400 ea.	green to clear Overlay
3155	250 ea.	ruby to clear Overlay
3156	500 ea.	ruby to clear Overlay
3157	875 ea.	ruby to clear Overlay
3158	225 ea.	pink to white to clear Overlay
3159	475 ea.	pink to white to clear Overlay
3160	95 ea.	ruby stained
3161	95 ea.	ruby stained
3162	95 ea.	ruby stained
3163	95 ea.	ruby stained
3164	65 ea.	ruby stained, with correct stopper
3165	200 pr.	ruby stained
3166	225 ea.	ruby stained
3167	175 ea.	clear Overshot
	275 ea.	blue Overshot
	275 ea.	pink Overshot
3168	275 ea.	blue Overshot
	275 ea.	pink Overshot
3169	85 ea.	
3170	65 ea.	
3171	325 ea.	green threads on green
3172	185 ea.	ruby threads on clear, engraved
3173	185 ea.	ruby threads on clear, with correct stopper

STOPPERS

A container that has its correct stopper often will double in value. The purchase of stoppers known to be Sandwich is an investment that will pay handsomely from time to time.

Photo No.	Clear	Clambroth (Alabaster)	Opaque White	Canary	Amber	Blue	Ruby	Amethyst	Green
3174	2–3 ea.								
3175	2–3 ea.								
3176 a	2–3 ea.				7 ea.				
b					5 ea.				
c					5 ea.				
3177	15 ea.				40 ea.	28 ea.		30 ea.	
3178	15 ea.					28 ea.		30 ea.	
3179	20 ea.								
3180 a	—								
b	15 ea.								
3181	15 ea.					50 ea.			
3182	15 ea.								
3183 a	7 ea.								
b	7 ea.								
c	5 ea.								
d	5 ea.								
3184	18 ea.								
3185	5 ea.								

Photo No.	Clear	Clambroth (Alabaster)	Opaque White	Canary	Amber	Blue	Ruby	Amethyst	Green
3186	4 ea.								
3187	4 ea.								
3188	4 ea.								
3189									875 pale green
3190 a	3 ea.								5 ea. pale green
b	4 ea.								7 ea. pale green
c	3 ea.								5 ea. pale green
3191					1000				
3192					5 ea.				
3193				10 ea.	5 ea.		20 ea.	25 ea.	
3194	3 ea.								
3195 a	—								
b	40 ea.								
c	35 ea.								
d	35 ea.								
e	35 ea.								
3196	18 ea.								
3197	20 ea.								
3198	30 ea.								
3199	40 ea.								
3200	20 ea.								
3201	6 ea.								
3202	4 ea.								
3203 a	—								
b	4 ea.								
c	4 ea.			10 ea.	15 ea.	15 ea.		15 ea.	
3204 a	8 ea.			20 ea.	20 ea.	25 ea.	50 ea.	25 ea.	60 ea. dark green
b	8 ea.								
3205	10 ea.								
3206 a	8 ea.			15 ea.					
b	8 ea.			15 ea.					
c	8 ea.		20 ea.		20 ea.				
3207	5 ea.			15 ea.	15 ea.	18 ea.			
3208 a	5 ea.			15 ea.	15 ea.	18 ea.			
b	8 ea.			15 ea.					
3209 a	8 ea.								
b	8 ea.			18 ea.		18 ea.			25 ea.
c	8 ea.			18 ea.		18 ea.		25 ea.	
d	8 ea.			20 ea.	20 ea.	25 ea.	50 ea.	25 ea.	60 ea.
3210 a	15 ea.			25 ea.					
b	15 ea.				35 ea.				45 ea.
c	15 ea.				35 ea.				45 ea.
3211		25 ea.				45 ea.			60 ea. custard
3212 a									50 ea.
b						35 ea.			
c						35 ea.			
3213	5 ea.			12 ea.	12 ea.	15 ea.		18 ea.	
3214	5 ea.				12 ea.				

Photo No.	Clear	Clambroth (Alabaster)	Opaque White	Canary	Amber	Blue	Ruby	Amethyst	Green
3215	5 ea.			12 ea.	12 ea.	15 ea.		18 ea.	
3216	8 ea.			18 ea.		18 ea.		25 ea.	25 ea.
3217	5 ea.			12 ea.	12 ea.	15 ea.		18 ea.	
3218 a	10 ea.								
b	12 ea.								
c	15 ea.								
d	15 ea.								

Photo No.		
3219 a	15 ea.	
b	18 ea.	
c	22 ea.	ruby threads on clear
d	12 ea.	
3220 a	15 ea.	
b	20 ea.	
c	15 ea.	
3221 a	20 ea.	ruby threads on clear
b	25 ea.	ruby threads on clear
c	20 ea.	ruby threads on clear
d	20 ea.	ruby threads on clear
3222 a	100 ea.	
b	110 ea.	
3223 a	90 ea.	
b	100 ea.	
3224	—	

BALLS

Photo No.		
3225	150	
3226	140	
3227	150 ea.	
3228	150	
3229	175	
3230	60	
3231	60	
3232	50	
3233 a	90	
b	—	
3234	500	with extension
3235	500	with extension
3236	160	
3237	15 ea.	
3238	12 ea.	
3239 a	12 ea.	
b	180	
3240	12 ea.	
3241	—	
3242	45 ea.	

COVERED CONTAINERS

Little value remains to a container that has lost its cover. Keeping covers in pristine condition guarantees maximum return on the dollar spent for containers.

Photo No.	Clear	Clambroth (Alabaster)	Fiery Opalescent	Opaque White	Canary	Amber	Blue	Amethyst	Green
3243	3500				6500		7500		
3244	350				500		600		
3245	4000				7500		8500		
3246	—								
3247	4000				7500		8500		
3248	—								
3249	350				500		600		
3250	3500				6500				
3251							9000		
3252	—								
3253	600	750		800	1200		1800		2800
3254	—								
3255				350			550		
3256				250					
3257				300					
3258				400 with cover					
3259					1200		1100	1200	
3260		1000		1500			2500		3500
3261 a		1000		1200			2000	500	
b		800		1000			1500	400	
c		600		800			1100	300	
3262		600		800			1100	300	
3263 a		1000					1800	950	
b	—								
3264		90							
3265	250						1600		2200
3266	300						1400		1800
3267 a	—								
b	300						1400		1800
3268 a	200	500					1200		1500
b	50	275					375		500
3269	250	350			900		900		1500
3270	300	375		450	1200		900		1500
3271 a	45	110		125	550		375		500
b	50								
3272	190 with cover						1000 with cover		
3273	90				875		1000		
3274	110			275					
3275	50								
3276	85 ea.			200 ea.	375 ea.				
3277 a	—								
b				50					
3278	425						1000	1000	
3279				300			575	650	
3280 a	110				300		575		575
b	110				275		525		525

Photo No.	Clear	Clambroth (Alabaster)	Fiery Opalescent	Opaque White	Canary	Amber	Blue	Amethyst	Green
3281	—								
3282 a	22	45			85		115		160
b	22	50			90		135		175
3283				150				180	
3284	85	180	200		225	250	325	375	
3285					325				450
3286	—								
3287							750		
3288	—								
3289	80	225			375		575		
3290	425 ruby to clear Overlay								
3291	65		110					225	
3292 a	40		125						
b	40		125						
3293 a	40		125				225		
b	40		125						
3294 a	40		125						
b	40		125				225		
3295			35						
3296				28 ea.					
3297			135						
3298			60						
3299	50 ea.	80 ea.		80 ea.	90 ea.		110 ea.	135 ea.	150 ea.
3300	—								

TOYS

Glass toys made during the Nineteenth Century were intended for children's play. Expect to find more roughage than is found on adult tableware. The value does not drop as rapidly when toys are chipped or damaged.

Photo No.	Clear	Clambroth (Alabaster)	Fiery Opalescent	Opaque White	Canary	Amber	Blue	Amethyst	Green
3301	400 with burner						875 with burner		
3302	450 with burner						1000 with burner		
3302 a	25						60		
b	475 with burner						1500 with burner		
3304	450 with burner								
3305	500 with burner						1200 with burner		
3306	1000 complete								
3307	70								
3308 a	100								
b	185								
3309	100								

Photo No.	Clear	Clambroth (Alabaster)	Opaque White	Canary	Amber	Blue	Ruby	Amethyst	Green
3310	250								
3311	450						600		
3312	250						500		
3313	250						500		
3314	250						500		
3315	425				1200				
3316	350 the set						1100 the set	1200 the set	
3317	250 the set		900 the set		700 the set		1000 the set	1100 the set	
3318	160 ea.		375 ea.		400 ea.		500 ea.	550 ea.	
3319	225 the set				600 the set		900 the set	950 the set	
3320	38 ea.	65 ea.	90 ea.		125 ea.		150 ea.	165 ea.	200 ea.
3321 a	38 ea.	65 ea.	90 ea.		125 ea.		150 ea.	165 ea.	200 ea.
b	40 ea.	75 ea.	125 ea.		165 ea.		250 ea.	250 ea.	225 ea.
c	38 ea.	65 ea.	90 ea.		125 ea.		150 ea.	165 ea.	200 ea.
3322	425								
3323	18 ea.				90 ea.	150 ea.	110 ea.	110 ea.	150 ea.
3324	18 ea.				90 ea.	150 ea.	110 ea.	110 ea.	150 ea.
3325 a	18 ea.				100 ea.	160 ea.	120 ea.	120 ea.	175 ea.
b	28 ea.				125 ea.	175 ea.	150 ea.	150 ea.	200 ea.
3326	28				90	160	120	120	175
3327	28				90	160	120	120	175
3328 a	28 ea.						125 ea.	175 ea.	
b	35 ea. pressed handle						150 ea. pressed handle	150 ea. pressed handle	175 ea. pressed handle
	75 ea. applied handle						275 ea. applied handle	275 ea. applied handle	300 ea. applied handle
3329	35 ea.	80 ea.					150 ea.	175 ea.	150 ea.
3330	200								
3331	100								
3332	100								
3333	85								
3334	38 ea.	100 ea.					150 ea.	175 ea.	200 ea.
3335	38						150		200
3336 a	100 ea.		250 ea.				550 ea.	600 ea.	700 ea.
b	65 ea.		200 ea.				450 ea.	475 ea.	500 ea.
3337	150 the set				400 the set		550 the set	600 the set	
3338	75	150	275		300		400	450	
3339	75	150	275		300		400	450	
3340	75	150	225		300	600	400	600	
3341	75 ea.	150 ea.	225 ea.		300 ea.	600 ea.	400 ea.	600 ea.	
3342	60								
3343	60								
3344	75 ea.	150 ea.	275 ea.		500 ea.		550 ea.	600 ea.	700 ea.
3345	300 ea.				900 ea.		1000 ea.	1000 ea.	1000 ea.
3346 a	150 ea.								
b	225 ea.								
3347	300 with underplate		875 with underplate		875 with underplate		1200 with underplate	1300 with underplate	1400 with underplate
3348 a	110 ea.		200 ea.		200 ea.		225 ea.	250 ea.	300 ea.
b	90 ea.		175 ea.		175 ea.		200 ea.	225 ea.	275 ea.
3349	75 ea.		125 ea.		125 ea.		200 ea.		
3350	75 ea.		125 ea.		125 ea.		200 ea.		
3351	150				500		750	850	1000

Photo No.	Clear	Clambroth (Alabaster)	Fiery Opalescent	Opaque White	Canary	Amber	Blue	Amethyst	Green
3352	150								
3353 a	40 ea.								
b	75 ea.								
3354	150								
3355	150 the set								
3356	200 the set with box								
3357	150 the set								
3358 a	15 with cap								
b	20 with cover								
c	18 with stopper								
3359	18 ea.				50 ea.				
3360	200 pr.		750 pr.		650 pr.		900 pr.	1000 pr.	1400 pr.
3361	150 ea.		275 ea.		600 ea.		600 ea.	600 ea.	600 ea.

Photo No.

3362	50 ea.	multi-colored
3363	150	opaque white
3364	500	clear
3365	7500	clear
3366 a	250	canary
b	650	Vasa Murrhina
c	700	ruby
3367	150	Vasa Murrhina
3368	150	ruby to clear Overlay
3369	—	
3370 a	125	clear
b	125	clear
c	100	clear
d	125	clear
3371	250 ea.	ruby to clear Overlay

CREATIONS OF NICHOLAS LUTZ

Photo No.

3372	—
3373	—
3374	—
3375	—
3376	—
3377	—
3378	—
3379	—
3380	—

Photo No.	
3381	—
3382	—
3383	575
3384	900
3385	1000
3386	1000
3387	750
3388	1400
3389	—
3390	600
3391	600
3392	575
3393	1200 pr.
3394	600
3395	175
3396	700
3397	700
3398	300
3399	2000
3400	160
3401	90
3402	300 ea.
3403	7500
3404	95 ea.
3405	700
3406	50
3407	—
3408	90–150 ea.
3409	90–150 ea.
3410	90–150 ea.
3411	90–150 ea.
3412	—
3413	100
3414	100 ea. with documentation
3415	15
3416	—
3417	—

CANDLESTICKS

A single candlestick is worth less than 50% of a matching pair. In most instances, a two-color candlestick is more valuable than the same candlestick made in one color.

Photo No.	Clear	Clambroth (Alabaster)	Opaque White	Canary	Amber	Blue	Amethyst	Green	Unusual Color
4001	2500 ea.								
4002	—								
4003	450 pr.								
4004	450 pr.								
4005	175 ea.								
4006	150 ea.								
4007	450 pr.								
4008	600 ea.					1500 ea.			
4009	3500 ea.								
4010	325 pr. including inserts			750 pr. including inserts			1400 pr. including inserts		

Photo No.	Clear	Clambroth (Alabaster)	Opaque White	Canary	Amber	Blue	Amethyst	Green	Unusual Color
4011	375 pr.								
4012	375 pr.								
4013	700 pr.								
4014	500 pr.								
4015	200 pr.			600 pr.		700 pr.			
4016	80 ea.			200 ea.					600+ ea.
4017	200 pr.			450 pr.					
4018	100 ea.			250 ea.		325 ea.			
4019	225 pr.			400 pr.					
4020	85 ea.			140 ea.		300 ea.			
4021	175 pr.			375 pr.			700 pr.		
4022	85 ea.			140 ea.			325 ea.		
4023	250 pr.	450 pr.		600 pr.	800 pr.	800 pr. blue and white		1200 pr. green and white	1400+ pr.
4024	175 pr.			400 pr.	550 pr.	550 pr.	700 pr.	750 pr.	
4025 candlesticks	250 pr.								
peg lamps	100 pr.								
4026	250 pr.			500 pr.		600 pr.	650 pr.		750+ pr.
4027	200 pr.	250 pr.		400 pr.	650 pr.	650 pr.	650 pr.	700 pr.	750+ pr.
4028	175 pr.			400 pr.	650 pr.	650 pr.	650 pr.	700 pr.	750+ pr.
4029	80 ea.			150 ea.		275 ea.	275 ea.		
4030	80 ea.			150 ea.		275 ea.	275 ea.		
4031	90 ea.			150 ea.					
4032	175 pr.	300 pr.	300 pr.	395 pr.	1000 pr.	550 pr.	600 pr.	750 pr.	800+ pr.
4033 a	95		500	950			1200		
b	125			1000			1500		
4034	—								
4035	—								
4036	90 ea.			140 ea.		250 ea.	250 ea.	300 ea.	400+ ea.
4037	90 ea.			140 ea.		250 ea.	250 ea.	300 ea.	400+ ea.
4038	125 ea.	175 ea.	200 ea.	325 ea.		400 ea. blue and white		800 ea. green and white	650+ ea.
4039 a	80 ea.					300 ea.		400 ea.	
b	125 ea.	175 ea.	200 ea.	325 ea.		450 ea.		600 ea.	500+ ea.
4040	125 ea.	175 ea.	200 ea.	325 ea.		450 ea.		600 ea.	500+ ea.
4041 a	175 ea.					500 ea. all blue / 450 ea. blue and white		650 ea. green and white	
b	150 ea.					350 ea. blue and white		500 ea. green and white	
c	175 ea.					500 ea. blue and white		700 ea. green and white	
4042	90 ea.			150 ea.	250 ea.	250 ea.	275 ea.	325 ea.	
4043	—								
4044 a	225		500		750	800	800	950	1000+
b	20								
4045	400		800		1200	1200	1200	1400	1500+
4046	125 pr.	225 pr.	250 pr.	600 pr.	800 pr.	900 pr.	1000 pr.	1000 pr.	1200+ pr.
4047	150 pr.	250 pr.	250 pr.	800 pr.	800 pr.	900 pr.	1000 pr.	1000 pr.	1200+ pr.
4048	200 pr.	300 pr.	400 pr.	800 pr.		1000 pr.	1200 pr.	1500 pr.	1600+ pr.
4049	800		2000	3500		4500	4500	5000	
4050		2000	2000	3000		4500	4500	5000	

Photo No.	Clear	Clambroth (Alabaster)	Opaque White	Canary	Amber	Blue	Amethyst	Green	Unusual Color
4051	125 ea.	175 ea.	200 ea.	225 ea.		300 ea.	300 ea.	400 ea.	
4052	200 pr.	400 pr.	450 pr.	800 pr.		800 pr.	800 pr.	900 pr.	
4053	90 ea.	150 ea.	200 ea.	225 ea.		300 ea.	300 ea.	400 ea.	
4054	350 pr.	650 pr.	700 pr.	900 pr.		1500 pr.	1500 pr.	2200 pr.	
4055	350 pr.	650 pr.	700 pr.	900 pr.		1500 pr.	1500 pr.	2200 pr.	
4056 a	125 ea.	275 ea.	300 ea.	400 ea.		600 ea.	600 ea.	800 ea.	
b						500 ea. blue and white		800 ea. green and white	
4057	—								
4058 a						550 ea. blue and white		875 ea. green and white	1200 + ea.
b	125 ea.	275 ea.	300 ea.	400 ea.		400 ea.	450 ea.	650 ea.	
4059						800 ea. blue and white, gilded			
4060	350 ea.					1200 ea. blue and white		2000 ea. green and white	
4061	300 ea.				700 ea.				
4062	—								
4063	140								
Fig. 5	500 ea. with socket								
4064	20								

INSULATORS

Photo No.			Photo No.	
4065	35–40	ea. with collar	Fig. 8	60
4066	90–110	ea. with cap and collar	4071	30
4067	16–20	ea. with collar	4072	—
4068	16–20	ea. with clamp	4073	250
4069	—		4074	—
4070	—		4075	—

OVERSHOT (FROSTED WARE)

Photo No.	Clear	Pink	Amber	Blue	Unusual Color
4076 a	200 ea.	700 ea.			
b	200 ea.	375 ea.			
4077	400 pr.	800 pr.		800 pr.	
4078	225 ea.	450 ea.			
4079 a	180 ea.	300 ea.			
b	160 ea.	280 ea.			
4080	75 ea.	250 ea.			
4081	75 ea.	280 ea.	450 ea.		
4082	90 ea.	250 ea.			

Photo No.	Clear	Pink	Amber	Blue	Unusual Color
4083	65–90 ea.	200–250 ea.			
4084 a	85 ea.	250 ea.		350 ea.	
b	135 ea.	300 ea.		350 ea.	
4085	125 ea.	250 ea.			
4086 a					240 ea. canary
b	110 ea.				
4087	75 ea.		135 ea.		
4088 a	75 ea.	135 ea.	150 ea.	175 ea.	
b	60 ea.	250 ea.		250 ea.	
c	60 ea.	200 ea.		200 ea.	
4089	95 ea.	135 ea.		175 ea.	350 ea. green
4090 a	160 ea.			300 ea.	
b	35 ea.			75 ea.	
4091 a	180 ea.			400 ea.	
b	160 ea.			300 ea.	
4092 a	100 ea.				400 ea. ruby
b	125 ea. amber handle			200 ea.	
4093	80 pr.	250 pr.			
4094 a	150 ea.				
b	140 ea.				
4095	150 the set	300 the set			
4096 a	45 ea.	135 ea.			
b	35 ea.	75 ea.			
c	75 ea.				
d	40 with stopper				
4097	25 ea.	65 ea.			
4098	90 ea.	160 ea.		200 ea.	
4099	65 ea.	110 ea.			
4100	135 ea.				250 ea. canary
4101	125 ea.				
4102	180 the set				
4103	75 ea.		160 ea.	175 ea.	
4104	35 the set	95 the set	110 the set	110 the set	
4105	35 the set	95 the set	110 the set	110 the set	
4106	110 ea.	225 ea.		250 ea.	
4107	300 the set				

VASA MURRHINA

Photo No.			Photo No.	
4108	300		4117	—
4109	—		4118	650
4110	90		4119	—
4111	—		4120	150
4112	450		4121	—
4113	100		4122	125
4114	110		4123	—
4115	—		4124	125
4116	160		4125	—

Photo No.				Photo No.			Photo No.	
4126	—			4128	—			
4127	—			4129	—			

4130–4155   Cut or engraved by N. Packwood in Sandwich, but not *manufactured* by Packwood.

4156–4176   Cut or engraved by J. B. Vodon and Son in Sandwich, but not *manufactured* by Vodon.

LATE BLOWN WARE

There are five levels of value.

- The price based on the type of article and its etched or engraved design.
- The addition of a monogram that cannot be traced back to the original owner of the article reduces the base price.
- The addition of a monogram with documentation that traces the object back to the original owner adds to the base price.
- A presentation piece that is completely documented, with a monogram, complete name, date, or special design, is valued significantly higher than any of the above.
- Colored pieces are very scarce and should be priced accordingly.

Photo No.		Photo No.		Photo No.	
4177	45	4206	150	4232	38
4178	20	4207	110	4233 a	125
4179	20	4208	185	b	25
4180 a	20	4209	20	4234	125
b	18	4210	22	4235	12 ea.
c	15	4211	15 ea. clear	4236	55
4181	20		85 ea. amber	4237	75 the set
4182	20	4212 a	10	4238	65
4183	25	b	12	4239	150
4184	55	c	12	4240	65
4185	165 for jar	4213 a	65	4241	50
4186	25	b	50	4242	65
4187	—	4214	5	4243	500 the set
4188	185	4215	85	4244	95
4189	800	4216	45	4245	250
4190	—	4217 a	100	4246	225
4191	40	b	15 ea.	4247 a	165
4192	40	4218	110	b	165
4193	35	4219	38	4248	125
4194	110	4220	200	4249 a	45
4195	50	4221	30 ea.	b	185 with drainer
4196	40	4222	365	c	55
4197	250	4223 a	55	4250	—
4198	—	b	65	4251	350 ea.
4199	20	4224	18	4252	18 ea.
4200 a	25	4225 a	10	4253	30 ea.
b	30	b	15	4254	18 ea.
c	30	c	15	Fig. 19	12 ea. clear wine
d	35	4226 a	10		50 ea. blue wine
e	50	b	10	Fig. 21	12 ea. clear wine
4201	3	4227	45		85 ea. green wine
4202	5	4228	65		
4203	65	4229	10		
4204	20 ea.	4230	10		
4205	65	4231	30		

4255–4260   Decorated by E. J. Swann in Sandwich, but not *manufactured* by Swann.

THREADED GLASS

Objects with colored threads on clear bodies have less value than objects with colored threads on colored bodies. The condition of the threads is critical to the value of the article. Etching and engraving adds to value.

Photo No.

4261	125	blue threads on blue
4262 a	250	ruby threads on clear, engraved
b	85	ruby threads on clear, engraved
4263 a	105	amber threads on amber
b	200	amber threads on amber
4264 a	125 ea.	amber threads on amber, engraved
b	250	amber threads on amber, engraved
4265 a	75	amber threads on amber, engraved
b	250	amber threads on amber, engraved
4266	65	blue threads on clear
4267	85 ea.	ruby threads on clear, needle etched
4268	50 ea.	clear threads on clear, engraved
4269 a	95 ea.	amber threads on amber, engraved
b	75 ea.	ruby threads on clear, engraved
4270	125 ea.	canary threads on canary, needle etched
4271	28 ea.	clear, no threads, engraved
4272	85 ea.	ruby threads on clear, engraved
4273	65 ea.	ruby threads on clear, engraved
4274 a	85 ea.	blue threads on clear
b	115 ea.	canary threads on canary
4275	50	ruby threads on clear, needle etched
4276	50	ruby threads on clear, needle etched
4277	400	ruby threads on clear, engraved
4278	110	ruby threads on clear, engraved
4279	75	ruby threads on clear

Photo No.

4280	200	ruby threads on clear
4281	240	ruby threads on clear
4282	125	ruby threads on clear, cased in white
4283	225	ruby threads on clear
4284	175	ruby threads on clear
4285 a	150 ea.	green threads on green
b	65 ea.	ruby threads on clear
4286	85	ruby threads on clear, etched
4287	65	ruby threads on clear, etched
4288	135	ruby threads on clear, engraved
4289 a	65	white threads on pink
b	95	white threads on pink
c	100	white threads on pink
4290 a	65	white threads on pink
b	95	white threads on pink
c	100	white threads on pink
4291 a	100	white threads on pink
b	150	white threads on orange
4292	95	ruby threads on clear
4293	135	ruby threads on clear
4294	—	
4295 a	35	blue threads on clear
b	135	blue threads on clear

4296	150	green threads on green
4297	140	ruby threads on clear
4298	200	ruby threads on clear
4299	85 the set	canary threads on canary
4300	40	ruby threads on ruby
4301	75 the set	blue-green threads on blue-green
4302	85 the set	ruby threads on clear
4303 a	100 the set	green threads on canary
b	35	ruby threads on blue
4304	85	ruby threads on clear

4305–4320 Decorated by Mary Gregory. Will be priced under *Lighting* and *Salt Shakers*.

EPERGNES

Because it is difficult to find completely assembled epergnes, they command high prices. Individual units and incomplete assemblies do not command high prices. Complete epergnes can be assembled by collecting individual units. The result is financially rewarding.

Photo No.

4321	700	
4322	750	
4323	40	base
	100	Frosted Madonna standard with fittings
	25	trumpet with fitting
	40	center plate
4324	150	Frosted Madonna standard attached to base, with fittings
	25	trumpet with fitting
	40	center plate

Photo No.

4325	300	Frosted Madonna standard attached to base, with fittings and center plate
	25	trumpet with fitting
4326	235	Frosted Madonna standard with fitting
	40	center plate
	300	Frosted Madonna standard attached to center plate, with fittings
	25	trumpet with fitting
4327 a	100	with fittings
b	235	with fitting
4328	—	
4329	10 ea.	
4330	5 ea.	
4331	235	Frosted Madonna standard with fitting, collar
4332	20	
Fig. 28	1000	Fish globe with hooks on standard
	800	Fish globe without hooks on standard
Fig. 29	125	clear
	200 +	color
Fig. 30	4500	with white opal globe
	5000	with blue opal globe
	6500	with lavender opal globe
Fig. 31	2200	
4333	875	

Photo No.			
4334 a	150	with fittings	
b	40	with fitting	
4335	800		
4336	800		
4337	25 ea.		
4338	25	three-hole	
	45	six-hole	
4339	750		
4340	150	three-unit assembly with fittings	
4341	600		
4342	40		
4343	500		
4344	100	with fitting	
4345	40		
4346 a	25	with fitting	
b	40	with fitting	
c	40	with fitting	
4347	750		
4348	100	with fitting	
4349	875		
4350	100	with fitting	
4351	50	with fitting	
4352	500		
4353	40 ea.	with fitting	
4354 a	65	with fitting	
b	35	with fitting	
c	50	with fitting	
Fig. 32	875		
4355	75	with rod and fitting	
4356	200	ruby threads on clear	
4357	40	with fitting	

SANDWICH CO-OPERATIVE GLASS COMPANY

Photo No.		Photo No.	
4358	500	4370	100
4359	500	4371	1200
4360	225	4372	325 pr.
4361	175	4373	30 ea.
4362	150	4374	125
4363	—	4375	250
4364	110	4376	225
4365	20	4377	225
4366	30	4378	250
4367	90	4379	95
4368	35	4380	165
4369	15	4381	90

TREVAISE

Photo No.

4382	900
4383	—
4384	1200
4385	950
4386	800
4387	600
4388	750
4389	—
4390	800
4391	—